ALSO BY MICHELANGELO SIGNORILE

Queer in America

OUTING YOURSELF

OUTING YOURSELF

How to Come Out as Lesbian
or Gay to Your Family,
Friends, and Coworkers

MICHELANGELO SIGNORILE

A FIRESIDE BOOK

Published by Simon & Schuster

NEW YORK LONDON TORONTO SYDNEY TOKYO SINGAPORE

FIRESIDE
Rockefeller Center
1230 Avenue of the Americas
New York, NY 10020

First Fireside Edition 1996
Published by arrangement with Random House, Inc.

FIRESIDE and colophon are registered trademarks
of Simon & Schuster Inc.

Manufactured in the United States of America

1   3   5   7   9   10   8   6   4   2

Library of Congress Cataloging-in-Publication Data

Signorile, Michelangelo, date.
Outing yourself : how to come out as lesbian or gay to your
family, friends and coworkers / Michelangelo Signorile.—1st
Fireside ed.
p.   cm.
1. Coming out (Sexual orientation)—United States.   2. Gay men—
United States—Family relationships.   3. Lesbians—United States—
Family relationships.   4. Gay men—United States—Social
conditions.   5. Lesbians—United States—Social conditions.
I. Title.
HQ76.3.U5S54   1996
305.9′0664—dc20   95-53991   CIP

ISBN 0-684-82617-8

To Rosemary Caggiano
and all other gay-supportive therapists

"IT'S OKAY FOR OTHERS,
BUT I COULDN'T POSSIBLY
COME OUT MYSELF"

Due to the work of mental-health professionals, gay activists, and much of the media, many people have learned that living their lives in "the closet" robs them of a full, rewarding life and forces them to live in fear and shame—even though they may initially have been in denial about the stress the closet creates for them.

But "coming out" of the closet doesn't necessarily mean telling everyone you run into that you are gay, lesbian, or bisexual. What it really means is no longer worrying about being "discovered" by friends, family, or coworkers.

Obviously you are in the closet if you are afraid to admit to yourself that you are gay or bisexual even though you are sexually attracted to people of your own gender. But if you have come out to yourself and still fear that someone will find out your secret, then you are still in the closet. Many of us—most of us, in fact—are out in some aspects of our lives but still closeted in others:

If you have come out to one or two heterosexual friends

or relatives, but have sworn them to secrecy, you are still in the closet.

If you have told a fair number of close friends and acquaintances but haven't been honest with your family—specifically your parents—you are still in the closet.

If you have told most of your friends and family about your homosexuality but have kept it secret from your coworkers—especially if you have allowed them to believe that you are heterosexual—you are still in the closet.

But if you have picked up this book, you don't want to remain in that closet. You have taken a preliminary step on the road to outing yourself.

You have probably come to the realization that living without lies and without fear of disclosure would be a liberating, powerful, wonderful thing to do, that being honest would make you feel better about yourself.

But you probably also believe that revealing your homosexuality to the people who know you and love you would be a horrifying, even dangerous action, one that seems completely out of the question for you. You may in fact be saying to yourself, "It's okay for others, but I couldn't possibly come out myself" or "It's fine for some people, but nobody understands me and my life" or "Nobody knows how utterly unacceptable it would be to tell my family, my friends, or my coworkers."

You probably feel that your situation is unique—and it is, everyone's is. You may believe that although other people have come out and continue to come out, it will always be impossible for you to come out fully.

You probably believe that your family, your friends, or your coworkers are far different from those of all the other people who've outed themselves.

You probably believe that when it comes to your

sexuality, the less your family and friends know, the better.

You may believe that it would be nice if they could accept you, if you didn't have to lie and live in secrecy, but that telling them the truth about yourself would be an utter disaster, one that would ruin whatever good relationships you have with them now, as well as deeply hurt them—or possibly even kill them.

These are all normal, natural feelings, genuine concerns that need to be taken seriously, worries or beliefs that are very strong and very real and should not be casually or quickly dismissed.

That is why the program for coming out of the closet this book puts forth has no time limit: The process may take you six months, five years, ten years, or a lifetime. The coming-out process is one of self-discovery, and each person has his or her own personal timetable, journey, and destination.

Outing Yourself provides preparation for the process, a guide for that journey, and a friend you can turn to for comfort when the going gets rough, which it will. But once you have decided that you will be happier not living in fear any longer, *Outing Yourself* will help you deal with the inevitable stress. Because the stress of coming out will never be as hard on you as the stress of staying in was.

Although many family members and friends often have less of a problem with homosexuality than we fear they will have, you can never predict how your own family and friends will react. This book cannot promise that they will unconditionally accept you, but it can prepare you for the various responses they may have and help you to deal with them honestly and openly.

Once you step outside the confines of your closet, you will find yourself at the beginning of a quest for inner peace and self-acceptance. No matter how others may respond to your homosexuality, you will always know that living in the closet is far more destructive than the trauma of coming out. For your own mental health and well-being, you have decided that you are now ready to come out. Do so, at your own speed and when you know it's safe.

Congratulations, and good luck.

FOREWORD BY
BETTY BERZON, PH.D.

The weekend of my fortieth birthday I arranged to be alone. I wasn't sure why I was doing that until Saturday morning, when I awoke from a dream in which I was running desperately from hotel to hotel looking for somewhere to check in, somewhere I was supposed to be. It was not immediately clear, but slowly I realized that the time had arrived to face the runner in the dream—to allow the quandary rather than flee from it, to seek while awake the elusive answer that drew me into the mad pursuit of my dream.

For eighteen years I had lived a heterosexual life, determined to overcome a brief foray into homosexuality in my early twenties. I lived in a closet elaborately furnished with satisfying work, a thriving social life, and romantic relationships with a lot of very decent men. On the outside I was no different from anyone I knew. On the inside I fought back the knowledge that I was different in one inescapably essential way.

During this weekend of coming out to myself I struggled with all the implications of accepting and integrating this alien part of my identity. Would I still be the same person? How would others feel about me? What would I do differently as a lesbian than I had done as a straight woman? Where would I meet other lesbians? Would I know how to act with them? When should I tell anyone? Who should I tell? What should I say?

I was reeling as these questions rapid-fired through my brain. I saw that I had a lot to learn, to adjust to, to work on, but the one thing that had somehow established itself, that I did not waver from, was that I was finished with subterfuge and self-deception. I was going to be authentic for the first time in my life, whatever it took, whatever changes I had to make. That was it—the end of trying to be something I was not.

I don't know why the weekend of my fortieth birthday became the crisis in which I outed myself, but there began a journey of many years in which I overtook the runner in the dream and settled us both down to a place where we absolutely are supposed to be. It wasn't easy. I uprooted myself and moved to another city. I see now that that was really not necessary, but this was before the Stonewall riots in New York in 1969, which ushered in the modern gay-rights movement and brought many men and women out of the closet: There were not then the myriad of gay and lesbian support services that have become available since, almost everywhere.

There was not a book like this one to guide me, to give me the structure to make sense of it all, to know what to expect and how to cope with the bandits, outside and inside, who would steal my courage and try to push me back into the closet. Like so many others who had to go through this process before help arrived, I winged it, made mistakes, acted the fool, calmed down, and finally got it. I didn't have to turn my life inside out. I was the same person I had always been, only better, more real, ready to love and be loved, willing to experience the newness of life without a cover.

I cannot emphasize enough the strength I have gained from becoming an open and honest gay person. I have been enabled, as a therapist, to reach out to countless men and women strug-

gling with the decision whether to come out or to come out further. I have listened to their fears, explored with them the minefields of family and career, watched them overcome inertia and disclose what seemed earthshaking only to find merely minor tremors and relief greater than they had ever imagined.

These experiences inspired me to translate the insights of my own self-discovery into two books: Positively Gay, New Approaches to Gay and Lesbian Life *and* Permanent Partners, Building Gay and Lesbian Relationships That Last. *In other forums—lectures, workshops, and media appearances—I continue to challenge gay and lesbian people to reinvent their lives, elevating pride over prejudice, raising the logic of the heart over fear of the unknown.*

I have been witness to the trend of people coming out earlier and earlier—not waiting until fortieth birthdays—using the support offered by college groups, even high school groups, gay and lesbian community agencies, and models of proud gay individuals such as the author of this book. Help for coming out has arrived in many forms, but the special value of this volume is its carefully designed step-by-step plan for making your way through the phases of outing yourself.

For many of us there had been no such preparation available for this most important experience of accepting, integrating, and disclosing our gay or lesbian identity. Mom and Pop were no help, because they were in the dark about it. As youngsters our peer group offered no support, because they either didn't know or didn't understand enough to get beyond their negative stereotypes. But times are changing. Gay is everywhere. They can't escape it, you can't escape it.

Being in the closet now is no longer the silent retreat it has been in the past. The activists are out there imploring you to emerge. The burgeoning gay and lesbian community lures you. The media have a newly found fascination with the lives of gay men and lesbians. You realize that you are one of many and that others have freed themselves from the imperatives of a fic-

tional identity. Your closet is becoming less a sanctuary, more an unacceptable constraint. You are ready to become known, heard, seen, and acknowledged for who you really are. With this book, you are in the right place to begin that process.

As I read through this text I am excited by the image of thousands of gay men and lesbians connecting with one another "on-line," through their computers. What a wonderful new frontier for exploring being gay, unraveling the dilemmas, supporting and guiding one another. Access becomes a magical concept—access to information, to contact with others like yourself, to the comfort of kinship. A line in Outing Yourself *sums it up: "To help others is really to help yourself, and to help yourself is really to help others."*

One of the chief virtues of this book is that its fourteen-step guidance program is based on the real stories of real people. As they are presented here, they are a varied lot, in age, background, and temperament. They represent the immense diversity of gay and lesbian people—no stereotype could possibly fit all of these folks. They are different from you and yet the same, because each must be the agent of his or her growth and change, just as you must be.

The voices that echo through these pages offer companionship in the struggle to honestly confront yourself and others. Coming out is not an event. It is a long path along which you will travel for the rest of your life, the trip becoming easier, the rewards more gratifying as you progress. But you must still be vigilant, because the heterosexual assumption will always be operating and you may, from time to time, have to correct the record: "There's nothing wrong with being heterosexual. It's just not what I happen to be."

This is a gentle book, easy to read and absorb—a primer for personal change. I believe it will be around for a very long time, because the need to come out, constructively, will be around for a very long time. I hope you will be inspired here to pursue your coming-out journey no matter what, and if you hit some rough patches in the road you will have this resource to help you keep going.

The freedom to be your natural self is elementary to your mental and emotional health, but you cannot achieve freedom as long as it is an abstraction. Only when you step into the reality of outing yourself can you begin to feel the potency of self-affirmation—the first heady signs of it all coming together in body, mind, and spirit—a fresh start, a vital new option.

CONTENTS

Preface   ix

Foreword by Betty Berzon, Ph.D.   xiii

Introduction   xxi

PART I   OUTING YOURSELF TO YOURSELF

Step 1. Identifying Yourself   3

Step 2. Recognizing Self-Loathing and Creating
          Self-Respect   12

Step 3. Learning the Truth About Being Gay   27

PART II   OUTING YOURSELF TO OTHER GAY PEOPLE

Step 4. Meeting Other Gay People   37

Step 5. Developing a Family of Friends   50

PART III   OUTING YOURSELF
TO YOUR STRAIGHT FRIENDS

Step   6. Telling Your Best Friend   59
Step   7. Coming Out to Other Friends   74

PART IV   OUTING YOURSELF
TO YOUR FAMILY

Step   8. That First Talk   83
Step   9. Keeping the Discussion Going   110
Step 10. Bringing Home Your Gay Friends and
          Partners   122

PART V   OUTING YOURSELF
TO YOUR COWORKERS

Step 11. Understanding and Assessing the Sexual
          Nature of the Workplace   137
Step 12. Letting Coworkers Find Out   147

PART VI   COMING OUT EVERY DAY

Step 13. Helping Others to Come Out   157
Step 14. Not Thinking About It at All   163

Acknowledgments   171

WHY OUT YOURSELF?

Every day, more and more lesbians and gay men are realizing that the continuing process of coming out dramatically improves the quality of their lives. We have come to realize that so many of the things that make our lives as lesbians and gay men miserable can be traced back to the closet. As mental-health professionals have long told us, the basic predicament of living like a second-class citizen and actively hiding the truth about ourselves diminishes our personal dignity and our self-esteem—even when we might not be aware of it—and our impaired self-esteem leads to many complex emotional problems.

Jonathan Rotenberg, a corporate strategy consultant who lives in Cambridge, Massachusetts, denied his sexuality throughout his teen years, burying himself in his work and his studies. He didn't date girls or have any interest in that regard; he thought he was just an "awkward" heterosexual. During college, after briefly wondering if he might be gay, he recoiled from the notion because homosexuality didn't fit in with the man he thought he wanted to be. "There was a tremendous amount of grief at that time," he told me when I interviewed him for my first book, *Queer in America*. "I would pour myself into work and try to ignore it. I kept giving myself warning signs that there was a dilemma, but I ignored them too and just kept punching away. A lot of problems developed, all of these irrational things: a fear of flying, just a total meltdown. I just was fighting this so hard."

Shelley, a twenty-three-year-old Baltimore college student, has come out as a lesbian to herself, has made some gay friends, and is dating a woman, but she hasn't told her family or any of her straight friends. She constantly feels a sense of shame, that she is doing something behind their backs. That pressure and stress take an enormous toll.

"I've always had a bit of a weight problem," Shelley says, "but it is exacerbated by stressful situations. Since I've been living this secret lesbian life, I've gained twenty pounds. I just eat myself into oblivion sometimes; I'm nervous and scared a lot of the time, and food becomes my escape valve. I know if I could just relieve the pressure, and just tell my parents and my sisters, a lot of this behavior would stop. And that's what I'm working toward."

The stories of Jonathan and Shelley, as well as those of the countless gay people who have come out (and the countless more who still struggle with issues of honesty and openness), attest to the ways in which the closet has been a destructive force in too many of our lives. For some people, like Shelley, the closet has aggravated or even created weight problems. In others, it has led to alcohol and drug abuse, depression, insomnia, phobias, stress, and other even more serious emotional disorders.

These emotional problems can then lead to or exacerbate physical disorders, such as hypertension, heart disease, stroke, and even cancer.

When they discuss how they came out, many people use the imagery of a great burden being lifted from them, that they feel like the free souls they were meant to be. This may not happen initially—coming out itself can be stressful and difficult, especially when family and friends react negatively—but in time most gay people say they are happier out of the closet than they were when they were in the closet. They feel better about themselves in general, and this positive outlook carries over into their day-to-day activities.

"Each time I tell someone new—a cousin, an old friend from school, or even a new friend at the gym—I get a certain kind of confidence boost," says Kathleen, a thirty-six-year-old Dallas advertising executive who recently came out to her family and is now planning to tell her coworkers. "It not only makes me feel better about myself, more honest and less secretive, but asserting myself in this way really gives me an overall self-assurance that carries through at work and even in my relationships. It's as if coming out is contagious: The benefits spread to every aspect of your life."

As Kathleen's comment illustrates, outing yourself changes your life in subtle ways that make you less afraid of the world around you and better poised to take on real challenges and lead a more productive, successful, and happy life.

Coming out of the closet is a process that gets you in touch with the real you, the person you were meant to be before you were forced to wear the mask of heterosexuality. Coming out means you no longer feel like a freak who must hide a terrible secret; instead, you feel like a normal person who is proud of who he or she is, the way normal people tend to be.

"The personal is the political," goes the old feminist adage. In many countries around the world today, coming out is also a political act—whether you are an explicitly political person or not. Being gay in the 1990s means being part of a large, diverse community of people who are under attack by people who don't understand homosexuality and are thus afraid of it. Beyond the personal reasons to come out, many gay men, lesbians, and bisexual men and women are also reaching the conclusion that they have a responsibility to a community of people, just as other groups—such as women, blacks, and Jews—feel an allegiance to their communities. These newly politicized bisexuals, lesbians, and gay men have decided that it is time to stand up and be counted, to be identified as part of a community, and to make gay people so familiar that they no longer induce fear. Coming out instills a sense of duty, a sense that you are helping your community in the most effective way possible: by giving it visibility.

Visibility itself builds self-esteem, and thus the process of coming out creates a powerful cycle in which the personal fuels the political, which in turn fuels the personal. Outing yourself brings you to an understanding of a simple but often overlooked fact of life: To help others is really to help yourself, and to help yourself is really to help others.

COMING OUT WISELY

While it is important for you to come out of the closet, it is equally important to come out in a *smart* way, which means making sure it is safe and making sure that you won't be in physical danger or risk losing your home or livelihood.

If, for example, you are a teenager with little money and are dependent on religious-fundamentalist parents who will immediately throw you out if they find out you are gay, it is probably not wise to come out to your family just yet.

If you live in a rough city neighborhood or rural area where you are absolutely certain that you will be physically harmed by a homophobic gang, you probably shouldn't risk coming out to friends and neighbors.

If you live in a place where you are not protected by law against discrimination in housing and employment and your boss or landlord is extremely antigay, and you are certain that he or she will throw you out of your home or job, you'd have to change some of your life circumstances in order to come out to neighbors and coworkers.

That said, however, many of us exaggerate such circumstances as a way of avoiding the coming-out process: We make the obstacles seem much worse than they are, because we don't want to face our own fears about telling others we're gay. The first seven steps of *Outing Yourself* will help you proceed with caution. By Step 7, not only will you see past the self-loathing that all gay people experience but you will also have others around you who can offer their perspective. You will then be able to judge for yourself if it is time to proceed to the next seven steps.

PLANNING FOR THE DAY

If after completing Step 7 you still feel it would not be wise to proceed in coming out to friends and family, you can take a break and plan for the day when you are able to move on and accomplish more. The teenager with the fundamentalist parents, for example, can wait until she is

Introduction

able to successfully live on her own. The gay man living in the rough neighborhood can save his money and plan for the day when he can leave and be able to live freely. The person with the antigay landlord or employer can plan on moving to another place or possibly getting a new job.

Planning for the day when you can come out—literally picking a day in the future and possibly even marking it down on a calendar—is a hopeful alternative to feeling locked in your closet. But if you are to grow into a strong sense of self-worth, you must, in time, come out fully.

This book is meant to be a manual for people at any stage of the coming-out process. The fourteen steps are meant to provide a structure that can make the process easier. Some readers who have already completed some of the steps will feel a need to move on to other steps quickly. Others will find it essential to begin at Step 1, Identifying Yourself, and move slowly and cautiously through the process. In any event, read through each of the steps: Very few of us have completed any one step as fully as we might like to think. Coming out is a lifelong process, and we can all benefit from going over the basics every now and then.

WHY STEPS?

Soon after the publication of my first book, *Queer in America*, a study of the closet and how it harms people, I began to receive hundreds of letters from gay men and lesbians who said they now realized their lives would be greatly improved if they came out of their closets. They wanted to know how to go about doing that.

I remembered my discussions with Jonathan Rotenberg, the Cambridge corporate-strategy consultant, when

I interviewed him for a chapter in *Queer in America* about the lesbians and gay men in the computer industry who are using technology to fight for gay rights and empower people to come out of their closets.

While he was still in high school, Rotenberg was at the forefront of the burgeoning computer industry. At the age of thirteen, in 1976, Rotenberg founded the Boston Computer Society, a group dedicated to helping people learn about the personal computer at a time when this technology was completely alien. Within a year, the society experienced a 300 percent growth in membership, from ten people to several dozen. Heading the society—whose membership would eventually top 31,000 worldwide—Rotenberg became a teenage CEO and was soon internationally famous. By the time he was nineteen, he had been on the front page of *The Wall Street Journal* and named one of the ten most eligible bachelors in Boston by the *Boston Herald*.

It was not until almost ten years later, however, that Rotenberg dealt with his closet. "I realized how similar homophobia was to computerphobia," he told me, only half joking. "I saw so many parallels. People who grow up with computers and are fluent in them have no fear of them at all. Similarly, people who grow up with gay people don't see what the problem is. I began to think about how in business school we were being trained to take on complicated problems. We have a whole set of techniques to do so. . . . I figured if coming out could be broken down into a series of little steps—rather than one big one—it would be easier for people."

Rotenberg's analysis was similar to what many other people have told me over the past several years, including several gay-supportive psychotherapists. I began to correspond with some of the many people who'd written me letters looking for help in coming out, and found that a surprising number of them were also seeking a step-by-step system.

"I would like a program that takes you through, a little at a time, without any timetable, but that is direct and forthright," wrote Bill, a thirty-five-year-old businessman who lives in a small Texas town. "A program that shows you how other people have dealt with this. Something that is understanding of the hell I'm going through but that will gently pull me along, step by step."

Karen, a seventeen-year-old high school student who lives in upstate New York, told me it would be a lot easier for her if she were empowered to view coming out as something she could do incrementally, rather than as a monumental, one-time task: "For me, at my age, this is all so scary. I would like to know that each day I could do something little, something that I could tell myself is a good thing and is part of my getting out of the closet. The way it looks right now, it's like this big thing you have to do all at once, so I don't even want to face it. I'd like to be shown a process that moves that way, a system for coming out. I want to be able to do something today, and then do something tomorrow, and then something the next day, and the day after, so that over time it's done."

Eventually, I culled a great deal of information from a diverse group of people, including the hundreds of lesbians, gay men, and bisexual men and women who'd written me letters, as well as those I reached out to on gay computer-bulletin-board services. I interviewed some people directly on the telephone. Others filled out a lengthy questionnaire; some of these people I later interviewed by phone as well. The questionnaire and interview subjects ranged from those who'd come out of the closet fully, to those who were only partly out, to those who were still deeply closeted. Because people were at very different steps of the coming-out process, I have changed all names and localities (for the latter, a comparable urban, suburban, or rural locale has replaced the true one).

In consultation with psychotherapists, I derived the steps and exercises in this book from the techniques and strategies that my lesbian and gay subjects had said worked best for them in their own coming-out processes. The key, in almost every successful coming-out story— whether the reaction to the coming out was positive or negative—was to have worked from a well-thought-out plan. *Outing Yourself* will help you devise that plan.

IF NEWS GETS OUT TOO SOON

Sometimes, however, the coming-out process does not work out according to your plan. Parents, friends, or coworkers might find out you are gay without your having told them. Suddenly you may feel powerless, as if they are using information against you, confronting you with it, making you feel bad for being gay. The important thing in such a crisis is to take the power back from them as quickly as possible. You can regain power by making yourself the most immediate and positive source of information on the subject.

If, for instance, your parents find out you are gay sooner than you would have liked, go directly to Step 8, That First Talk, and follow this advice as closely as possible:

Do not deny you are gay or appear sorry or unhappy about it.

Above all, do not apologize. After all, how can you expect them to accept it when you seem sad and distraught about it yourself?

Sit them down and tell them what you already know about your homosexuality.

Dispel their myths, and answer as best you can any questions they may have.

If you are inadvertently found out by friends or coworkers, follow the same advice and go directly to those steps in *Outing Yourself* that apply to friends and coworkers. This may be exceedingly difficult. You may not have acquired all the necessary information you need and you may not have built the support groups that become vital, but with a lot of deep breaths and calm sense you can rise to this difficult occasion.

The best approach, of course, is to make sure people don't find out until you are ready to tell them. While this is usually within our control, we sometimes trip ourselves up: It is not uncommon to inadvertently leave hints around so that people find out without our having to tell them. It may be tempting, but being direct is usually better. For instance, do not leave this book on your desk until you are actually ready to let your coworkers know you are gay and until you are actually ready to discuss it with them.

Remain in control of information about yourself.

Be smart—and be careful.

While you must proceed with caution as you out yourself, always be aware that you are embarking on an exciting and rewarding journey. Try to enjoy it. Coming out may be difficult and stressful at times, but it is a rebirth. You are at the very beginning of a new life, one in which you will, for the first time in a very long time, be able to live in freedom, honesty, and pride.

PART I

OUTING YOURSELF
TO YOURSELF

IDENTIFYING YOURSELF

Perhaps you have had one or two homosexual experiences. Perhaps you've merely thought about it. Neither scenario necessarily means that you have told yourself you are gay.

Such thoughts and actions don't actually mean a person *is* gay. In some cases a heterosexual person, particularly an adolescent, may simply be experimenting—mentally or physically.

"People may be experimenting and seeing where their sexuality lies," notes Dr. Richard Isay, a clinical professor of psychiatry at Cornell Medical College and the author of *Being Homosexual*. "However, if someone has persistent homosexual experiences—and not necessarily encounters but day dreams and night dreams—and has had them for a long time, then that person is gay."

Some people are truly bisexual, equally attracted to both sexes. "I was always really turned on by men," says Sheila, a thirty-six-year-old rural Tennessee health-care worker.

Then in my early twenties I realized I was also really turned on by women. At first I thought I must be a lesbian, but my realization that I liked women did not stop or cover up my strong sexual attraction for men. I've accepted that I'm really bisexual, and I realize there aren't many people like me.

The vast majority of people who have recurring homosexual thoughts or experiences, however, are truly homosexual, although they often don't want to face the fact. Society has placed such a terrible stigma on homosexuality that even *thinking* about sex with someone of the same gender can be frightening. After having had several homosexual experiences, many people still deny that they are gay. They tell themselves that they are really heterosexual, they continue to live as heterosexuals, and they maintain that their homosexual incidents or thoughts don't and can't mean anything. Perhaps they tell themselves that they are bisexual as a way of holding on to some form of heterosexuality, some form of what they have been told is "normal" and "right." This is common, and has made many homosexuals—once they have fully come out—unfairly suspicious of the existence of true bisexuals.

Rudy, a twenty-four-year-old northern California law student, remembers how he couldn't face the truth when at age eighteen he began to realize his homosexuality.

I had what I guess you could call a crush on a guy at school—I mean I used to dream about kissing him—and every time I saw him in class my heart would start pounding and I'd turn red. I would then get this queasy feeling in my stomach, like I was sick, because this feeling of liking the guy made me ill, because I thought homosexuality was disgusting.

I convinced myself that I was bisexual, and that I could control the gay side and not act on it. But I soon realized that I didn't like girls in a sexual way at all. Two years later I began dating a girl who really was bisexual—I mean, she liked girls and guys and had had relationships with both. And, well, she and I had very little sex. After a lot of long talks she eventually said to me, "You're not bisexual. You're gay."

I went home that night, and for the first time wrote in my journal, "I'm gay." Then I crossed it out. I just couldn't face it.

DECADES SPENT WITHOUT IDENTIFYING ONESELF AS GAY

For some people, this first step of identifying oneself as gay or lesbian (or even bisexual) can take many years to complete. Doris, a fifty-four-year-old Buffalo, New York, business owner, married a man and had four children before eventually coming out as a lesbian and divorcing her husband—after thirty years of marriage. "Ever since I can remember, I wanted to be near women, to be physically close to them in a way that I really never wanted to be with men—even though I forced myself to be with men in that way," she says.

I admitted those feelings to myself for a very long time. But still, in those days that didn't matter. If you wanted to do well, you got married. Besides, I wasn't able to deal with the feelings anyway. They were too frightening, too eerie and weird, you know?

Then, after years of just barely acknowledging to myself that I had a longing to be intimate with a woman, I finally did experience it with a very close friend who was also married. But to actually identify

myself as a lesbian? Oh God. No, it was years and years
before I could actually do that.

"From the moment one begins to suspect that one
might be 'different' from others the seed of doubt is sown,
sending out corrosive roots to obstruct and inhibit the
process by which self-esteem naturally grows," declares
author and journalist Mark Thompson, who has written
much about the coming-out process and the dynamics of
gay life. Thompson stresses the notion of "coming out
inside," coming out to oneself. "There's a valuable part of
ourselves that was stolen at an early part of our lives," he
says, "and we need to get it back. The doubt is sown deep
inside of us because society still carries the message that
being gay is bad. We internalize all of that."

UGLY WORDS

Because of the social stigma attached to them, the mere
words "gay" and "lesbian"—not to mention "homosexual," "fag," "dyke," and "queer"—are terms that most
people don't want associated with themselves. It's amaz-
ing how powerful these words can be. Some people
engaging in sex with people of the same sex, many even
in their first same-sex relationship, still cannot bring
themselves to say that they are lesbian or gay. For some,
the reluctance is subtle: They get around such identifica-
tion by saying that they shun "labels" of any kind and
don't like "categorizing" themselves. For others, the
unwillingness to identify themselves as lesbian or gay is
more conscious, tinged with internalized homophobia.

"I liked being with guys and having sex with guys, but I
kept telling myself that I wasn't 'gay,' or a 'fag,' or any of
that," recalls Ramon, a twenty-six-year-old Miami sales
clerk.

My family is Cuban, and in our culture being macho is very important. So I'd tell myself that I was every bit a man, and that the men I was sleeping with and hanging out with were real men—we just had sex with each other, that's all. "Gay" was something else.

To me, it was all the stereotypes—effeminate men, drag queens, you know. I wouldn't have sex with someone who identified themselves as "gay." I believed that if I didn't say I was that—even to myself—then I wasn't.

BEGINNING A JOURNEY

Ramon's experience resonates for many gay men and lesbians who refuse to accept their homosexuality. But many people who think they accept their newfound homosexuality have never really identified themselves as gay or lesbian. Self-identifying is a way of starting the coming-out process: You can't tell other people that you're lesbian or gay until you've told yourself. It's also important to identify yourself as gay as a way of rejecting the hatred directed at you and the lies told about you. Identifying yourself starts you on a long journey.

"I first identified myself as gay when I was about twelve or thirteen years old," says Lincoln, a nineteen-year-old West Virginia college student.

It was a scary situation but one that sticks out permanently in my mind. I was in my bathroom, brushing my teeth, looking at myself in the mirror. All of these feelings I had been having but not really understanding were flooding into my mind while I looked at myself— all of these thoughts about men and a kind of realizing I was a homosexual. I began to cry, and then I prayed to God to change me because I thought it was evil or wrong. But then, from that point on, I underwent a tremendous inner healing. From the "mirror incident" I learned to accept for myself that I would not be changed; I was gay.

Lincoln's "mirror incident" is something we can all learn from. By looking himself in the mirror and facing the truth about himself, no matter how painful, Lincoln was able eventually to find inner peace and come to terms with his homosexuality.

The following exercise is the first of many in this book. These exercises are based on the actual experiences of many lesbians and gay men who, like Lincoln, stumbled upon some rituals that helped them. Depending on where you are in your coming-out journey, you will either want to read the exercises and think about them or actually *do* them. But this overall process is about coming out: Actions will help you more than words, and words will help you more than thoughts.

EXERCISE 1: "MIRROR, MIRROR"

Go to your bathroom mirror. Pick a time when you know there is no one around and when you know for sure that no one will walk in on you or hear you. Run the water in the sink if you want to be really sure no one will hear you.

Look at yourself in the mirror and study your face. Take a few minutes to get to know yourself and your face in the mirror. Feel good about this person who is taking charge of himself or herself.

When you are ready, say softly and sweetly "I am gay" or "I am a lesbian."

Say it slowly, over and over again, no matter how painful it is, no matter if it makes you cry. As the gay film historian and activist Vito Russo once said, "The truth will set you free, but first it will be a pain in the neck." Hear the truth, and accept the pain, which will eventually subside. For now, feel it and don't hold in your grief.

Mourn the fact that you are not the person you thought you were, the person everyone else wanted you to be. Think about that person and think about all the things about that person that did not represent the real you.

Say goodbye to the old you forever, someone who helped you out through thick and thin. This may be a sad experience, but it is time for that person to go. Eventually, you will celebrate the real you, the person you are now allowing to come out.

"Basically, coming out is a death and rebirth experience," says author Mark Thompson. "To come out, something has to die—whatever it was you thought you were. That's a painful experience. In a sense, you're killing a former constructed identity and creating a new one."

Do Exercise 1 as often and as long as you feel necessary, then go on to Exercise 2.

EXERCISE 2: "I AM WHAT I AM"

After you have done Exercise 1 a few times, go to a quiet, private place where no one will walk in on you—the woods or a park, if you have to—and bring a pen and paper. For this first time that you are doing Exercise 2, divide the paper lengthwise into three columns. In the left-hand column, beginning at the top, you will write "I am gay" or "I am a lesbian."

I am gay
I am gay
I am gay
I am gay

Then, next to that phrase, in the middle of the column, write down a negative word that describes homosexuals—one of the many ugly words that you have heard over the years from your family, your friends, or even your teachers. Go down the page, writing down another ugly epithet next to "I am gay" or "I am a lesbian."

I am a lesbian	dyke
I am a lesbian	lezzie
I am a lesbian	butch
I am a lesbian	diesel

Read all of the words you have in the middle column over and over again. Face the words that are used against you, desensitize yourself to them, and move on. After you have read the words several times, fold the paper and put it somewhere inside this book. (You will use this piece of paper again, in Step 2.)

The next time you do Exercise 2, divide the paper into two, not three, columns. Simply write down the words "I am gay" or "I am lesbian" in the left-hand column and the epithets on the right. As you write the words, accept them as a description of the new you. As in Exercise 1, say goodbye to the old you and feel the accompanying pain and grief.

Each time you finish this exercise, rip up the paper and throw it away. But remember to keep the three-columned paper you have folded and put in this book.

NO TIMETABLE

Do Exercises 1 and 2 until there is little or no pain associated with the epithets or with saying goodbye to the old you. You will know when you are ready to move on.

You may not feel good about yourself yet, but that will

happen in time, after several more steps in the Outing Yourself process. The goal of this first step is for you to face the truth, to verbalize it and write it down. You'll know it's time to move on when the grief you've experienced is replaced by a desire to move and grow and change, an urge fueled by excitement and/or trepidation.

RECOGNIZING SELF-LOATHING AND CREATING SELF-RESPECT

Some people would have you believe that abhorring homosexuality is "instinctual" behavior among most of the population. That is the big myth. Hatred of homosexuals is no more natural than hatred of blacks or hatred of Jews.

While most people are not attracted to people of the same sex, the outright disgust and fear that many people harbor for homosexual acts is instilled in them from a very young age by our society. If society stopped teaching people to revile homosexuality, most heterosexuals would view homosexuality the way that homosexuals view heterosexuality: something that just doesn't interest them.

Since the vast majority of people are heterosexual, learning to hate homosexuality causes them little if any internal conflict—at least until their friends and loved ones come out. But for those of us who are homosexual, society's teachings cause much conflict internally. Unlike everyone else, from the day we realize that we are gay, our attempts to process society's antigay attitude lead to emotional conflict and psychological damage. Plus, we feel compelled to keep our conflict a secret.

Society teaches us that there are grave consequences for us if we do not keep our sexuality hidden, that we will pay a price if we come out of the closet. We are threatened with the destruction of our livelihood, our lives, and even our souls. We are taught that we will be scorned and ridiculed. We are made to believe that we will lose our jobs, our homes, our families, that we may put our very lives in danger.

Staying in the closet, on the other hand, is rewarded in our society. Gay men and lesbians learn that if they want to be loved by family and friends, and if they want to make it in business and career, they must pretend to be heterosexuals. The closet is thus firmly embedded in all of our cultural, political, and social institutions. It exists at home, at work, at school, and even on television. For most of us, there is no escaping its overwhelming power.

In that way, the stress that the closet imposes on each of us as individuals cannot be overestimated. It often robs us of a happy, fulfilling life, forcing us to live a lie and tremble with fear, afraid that we will one day be exposed. Put simply, the closet is dangerous, and staying inside can often lead to dire consequences.

"I was always depressed as a teenager, for a lot of reasons that had to do with low self-esteem, not feeling I was pretty, and being subjected to racism sometimes, but when I realized I was a lesbian, that was the last straw for me," says Julie, a thirty-three-year-old Minneapolis waitress.

> I think being black and being a lesbian or a gay man is harder in a way. It's not that black people are more homophobic than whites, but I think racism makes some black people look at it differently. A lot of black

people who are pretty accepting and might actually be cool about it under different circumstances don't like when you go public because it's like they're afraid of what kind of image it portrays of blacks, that it makes it look like blacks are more likely to be "queer" or something.

When a lot of black gays and lesbians first figure out they're homosexual, they think it just can't be true because the little bit that they even see of gays and lesbians in the newspapers, on TV, and in the movies is about white gays, so until they find the black gay political organizations and social groups and nightclubs and whatnot, they think they're selling out or something just for having those feelings.

I know I kind of felt that at first. And a lot of homophobic black straight people try also to make you believe that it's a white thing.

Julie was sixteen when she first realized her lesbianism and plunged into a deep depression.

There was a girl at school who was real butch, you know, very masculine and with short hair, and everyone at school would be calling her "dyke" and she would just give them the finger. I thought she was so cool. I couldn't figure out why I liked her, but I wanted to hang with her.

So I did. I became friends with her. Then, after a while, it happened—we had sex. And then I was totally crazy. Cried for days and would not talk to her or meet with her again. I just told myself that this was it—my life was finished—because I knew I couldn't be, you know, "normal"—I mean what I'd been told was "normal"—and get married and have kids, because I knew I just was not interested in having sex with a man.

Driven by self-loathing, Julie did what far too many gay men and lesbians have done at one time or another: She attempted suicide.

> I took a whole bottle of my stepfather's sleeping pills. But they found me on the floor, sick, and I wound up in the hospital getting my stomach pumped. It got things out in the open, forced my mother to deal with it and get me some professional help, but it was a dumb way to do it.
>
> After I was seeing a therapist for a while, and after my mother and stepfather talked it over with me and with the therapist, and after I found so many other lesbians who'd been going through the same stuff, things got a lot a better and I felt supported. I realized that this was what I should have done from the beginning: Look for help, talk to people, read up on the subject, and not keep it all bottled up.
>
> I would say to people going through the same thing that it's so much easier if you deal with it and look for the help yourself rather than do something drastic and dumb—like what I did.
>
> There are so many loving people out there who want to help. And the fantasy world where there are people just like you, where people do accept you, really does exist. You just have to find it.

THE ORIGINS OF SELF-LOATHING

Self-loathing can lead you to self-destruction. Conversely, self-respect leads to self-enrichment, which is what you are striving for. Like Julie, you too may have found yourself at rock bottom. And, like Julie, you may have contemplated or attempted suicide. If you have not yet begun to battle the self-loathing that you have experienced all your life, you may still have those thoughts now.

When you are consumed by self-loathing, you experience a sense of powerlessness and hopelessness. You may feel as if you cannot live any longer unless conditions "out there" change, and yet you sense that it will be impossible to make those conditions change. What you must understand—and tell yourself over and over again—is that while you cannot change conditions "out there," you can attack the feelings inside that are causing you to feel this way. You can fill yourself with self-respect—no matter how many people hate homosexuals, no matter who hates you for being one.

And once you are filled with self-respect, no matter how insurmountable your problems seem, you will never think about self-destruction again.

Before you successfully confront self-loathing, however, you must understand where it comes from. Self-loathing is imposed upon you by the most well-intentioned and inspirational people and institutions in your life: your family, your school, even your house of worship. This is itself difficult to accept: Who wants to believe that the people who love you most—the people who have been most important in your life—would do something bad to you? How, you ask yourself, could the people who care most about you want to make you feel so terrible that you have contemplated destroying your life? These questions are so difficult to comprehend that we dismiss them and begin to tell ourselves that *we* are the ones with the problem, that our homosexuality—which we did not choose—is what's wrong. It is precisely at that moment that we cave in to self-loathing: *I must be really awful to make them think so ill of people like me. I must never let them know the truth.*

THE VICTIMS OF HOMOPHOBIA

The best way to understand how hatred becomes self-hatred is to think of homophobia as a *disease*, similar to alcoholism and drug abuse—afflictions that cause people to behave in irrational ways, even as they are often in denial about what they are doing and saying. Thus it becomes easier to understand that the people we love can be homophobic. Like the people we know and love who may be alcoholics or drug abusers, they don't mean to hurt us, but they do. They are driven by an ugly disease. We must have compassion for them and understand how familial predisposition and societal pressures have caused them to behave and think in the manner in which they do, and we should summon up the courage and patience to deal with their disease. *But we must not allow them to harm anyone, emotionally or physically, especially ourselves.*

Though we may love and care for someone who is an alcoholic, we would not allow that person to get behind the wheel of a car while intoxicated and we would certainly not let that person drive while we were in the car. Similarly, we must not allow those whom we love who happen to be homophobic to make us feel terrible about ourselves, so terrible that we think about taking our own lives.

Most of us know only a few (if any) people who are alcoholics or drug abusers. In the case of homophobia, however, it is possible and probable that almost everyone around us is afflicted. We cannot let this lead us to believe that *they* are the healthy ones simply because they outnumber us. Homophobia is a widespread affliction, and homophobia is an epidemic. But homophobia is curable.

Like other diseases, homophobia is also, unfortunately, contagious. Parents, teachers, and clergy pass it on to their children and those they influence. When the children are gay, it is passed on as internalized self-loathing.

Once you view homophobia as an affliction suffered by your parents and others, an affliction they have passed on to you, you begin to recognize that they don't know that their homophobia is destructive for you as well as for all gay people. You will find it easier to continue to love your family while at the same time understanding that they have a problem that endangers your emotional well-being. You can be patient and understanding with them, but you must empower yourself to feel good about being gay in spite of what they may say or do. You must firmly resolve, right now, that even if they have passed this disease on to you, you are going to rid yourself of it and not allow it to eat away at you.

HOMOPHOBIA AND RELIGIOUS INSTITUTIONS

Sadly, homophobia infects even our most spiritual institutions—institutions some of us have been told are divine and infallible. No matter how intricately woven homophobia is into the beliefs of your faith, no matter how many biblical passages or church decrees you are told about (in Step 3 you will learn how to counter some of these passages and decrees), you can come to understand that religious leaders can be as sick with homophobia as anyone else. Often they will look for validation and support to enable their disease, much as alcoholics look for people who will enable them and tell them it's okay to have another drink or that they do not have a drinking problem. The religious leaders will select certain quotes from the Bible or decrees from still other religious leaders who are just as afflicted with homophobia. They do not realize how they are harming you, perhaps far more than even your parents ever could. If they could see things clearly, they would realize that there are doctrines of their faith by which they could embrace you and accept you. Many religious leaders are friendly to gay people and lovingly accept them. (Step 4 will help you find them.)

"I couldn't stand myself because I believed that it was my fault, that I was giving in to evil, that I was a deviant and a terrible human being," remembers Arthur, a twenty-seven-year-old Chicago political consultant. Arthur grew up in southern Georgia; his parents were originally Catholics and later became born-again Christians.

> Homosexuality was discussed in my house quite a bit— it was evil, terrible, wrong, and perverse. There was no compromise. If you were a homosexual, you were a sinner and among the worst kind. The only thing you could do was repent and ask God for mercy.

It was at fifteen that Arthur first thought he might be gay.

> These feelings that I now realize had always been there, even when I was four or five, began bubbling up—this desire to just be close to boys—specific boys I knew— and just touch them and hold them. Rather than seeing it as something beautiful, which I should have been able to do, just as when many straight people begin to realize their sexuality, I could only react to these thoughts with horror because of what I'd been taught.

Throughout his high school years, Arthur says he spent most of his time alone.

> The guys at school, I don't know, I just didn't feel like them, and it made me feel worse to hang around them because I knew I was different. Deep down I knew I was

gay, and the thought revolted me. I didn't want to be
near anyone, especially guys, because sometimes they
would turn me on. I'd want to get close to them—and
that feeling made me hate myself. I kept trying to figure
out ways to get it out of me. Being alone was one way
to at least not face it.

When he was nineteen, Arthur had his first sexual experience with another man.

I felt guilty after it was over, even though I know I
enjoyed it. It took me years to realize that there was
nothing shameful about how I felt, that it was natural
and it was how I was supposed to be, and that God
would never condemn me for that. Once I realized that,
and saw that many gay people were wonderful human
beings, I accepted who I was, and I began to stop hating
myself.

It meant reading a lot and getting to know the gay
culture and seeing what the reality was, and how it was
different from what I'd been taught. I needed to get to
know the kinds of gay people I'd always been taught to
hate—the more flamboyant guys and the drag queens
and the very masculine kind of lesbians—and see that
they were normal, caring, often wonderful people and
not at all the "dangerous" people that society makes
them out to be. At the same time, I needed to meet
many gay people like me, run-of-the-mill average Joes,
and see that there were many like me and that the gay
community really is made up of quite a mix of America, and that gays are in every class and occupation and
of every race.

When I look back, part of the way I fought self-
loathing in the beginning, and came to love myself and
love gay people, was by envisioning what I'd like the
gay community to be, by thinking of all the good things

in life and good people in life that I'd like gays to represent—and then going on to find out that the picture I fantasized was not only true, but that gay people were what I'd envisioned and more. That was a cathartic experience, and you can't turn back to hating yourself after that.

SELF-LOATHING IS COMMON

Arthur's early feelings are shared by many people. You may have experienced them yourself. (You may still be feeling them now.) Battling self-loathing is a years-long process. We weren't taught to hate homosexuals in one day; undoing that hatred can't happen overnight.

The first step toward battling self-loathing is to identify it, admit to it, and understand that it is common, even *normal*, to hate yourself: *Every* gay person has grappled with internalized homophobia. In this way, you will understand that you are suffering from a disease too—not *homosexuality*, as some would have you believe, but *self-loathing*—and that though you may feel fine, a lot of what you believe about gay people is hazardous to your health. Arthur alludes to this when he says that he needed to get to know the kinds of gay people he'd always been taught to hate. You too have been taught to hate gay people, and while you might not think so now, the dislike you may have for gay people who dress a certain way or act a certain way is your self-loathing at work. It too must be confronted.

BEYOND HOMOPHOBIA TO AN ACCEPTANCE OF DIFFERENCE

Many gay people were so psychically damaged when they were young that they still suffer greatly from the disease

of self-loathing even after having been out of the closet
to friends, family, and coworkers for many years. In the
most extreme cases, they become quite vocal. They will
often lash out at the transgendered members of the gay
community, people who march in gay pride parades or
celebrate by dressing wildly, and political activists. Often
they charge that society's homophobia is the fault of those
gay people who are outspoken and visible. In essence,
what they are doing is directing their own internalized
homophobia outward onto other gay people.

This attitude is very common, and you may share it.
You may believe, for example, that drag queens, effeminate men, and butch lesbians give the community a bad
name and cause straight people to dislike gays even more.
You may think that if gays were to show that they are just
like everyone else they would be more accepted. This is
the externalization of your own internalized homophobia.

You should fight this response. First and foremost, we
gay people—like all people—should tell the truth about
who we are. We should let it be known that many of us
look like the average straight person next door. But we
must not hide the fact we are a diverse community, made
up of many sexual minorities, and that all of us, however
different from the norm, have the right to be visible.
Often, in fact, it is the people who are more flamboyant
and outspoken who force heterosexuals to confront their
own homophobia—even if at first their flamboyance
makes heterosexuals uncomfortable. Ever since the riots
at Stonewall that ushered in the gay-rights movement, it
has been the more extreme and loud gay people who have
secured much of our progress and cleared a safe space for
gay people of all stripes.

Those among us who appear more extreme have often
had lives tougher than those gay people who fit in more
easily. They were the ones who got tagged as "faggot" or

"dyke" when they were young, and they were the ones whose psychological nature or innate bravery required them to be forthrightly gay. If you are one of these stand-out types of gay people, it is important not to be bitter at those who more easily fit in, to have patience with them, and to empathize with the self-loathing they experience. Conversely, if you are someone who can operate unobtrusively in the world, it is important that you accept and get to know those who are different from you and realize that *your discomfort with certain gay people is a product of your own homophobia.*

Acknowledging and understanding self-hatred is the easy part. Fighting it off is the hard part. It requires enormous perseverance.

"DEPROGRAMMING" YOURSELF

"Deprogramming ourselves is a long and arduous process," wrote noted lesbian psychotherapist Betty Berzon in her book *Positively Gay.* "In our formative years we were all exposed to the same antigay jokes as our non-gay counterparts, the same stereotypes of lesbians and gay men, the same misinformation from our peers. For we gay and lesbian people who have swallowed all of this toxic material, it works against us from the inside, while society's homophobes work against us from the outside."

Deprogramming yourself is a lifelong process and is a major part of battling self-loathing. In this way, Step 2 is never completed fully. We spend our entire lives overcoming the self-hatred that society sears into us. The ability to *recognize* instances of self-loathing will help you refrain from behaving self-destructively, or acting in a homophobic way toward other gay people. That will happen in conjunction with Step 3, Learning the Truth.

You cannot complete further steps unless you are in

touch with your self-loathing and committed to fighting it. Self-loathing not only affects how you think about gay people but also clouds all of your decisions about when and how to tell friends, family, and coworkers that you are gay. Self-loathing will make you believe certain steps in the process are insurmountable when they are not. Self-loathing will keep you from moving on.

EXERCISE 3: MEDITATING ON SELF-RESPECT

The following Meditation Notes deal with this chapter's main points. They are a few basic truths about homosexuality designed to deactivate your self-loathing.

Find a quiet place where you can think without distractions.

Read each of the notes and let its meaning sink in.

Think of the stories of Julie and Arthur and others who have been battling self-loathing. Push yourself to understand, believe, and follow through on what the notes tell you.

At any point in the Outing Yourself process, whenever you feel confused, come back to the Meditation Notes. Find a quiet place and read them out loud. Do this exercise as often as you need to. Photocopy these notes and carry them with you. Look to the Meditation Notes as a set of rules for you to strive to live by. Make up some meditations of your own.

MEDITATION NOTES

- Self-loathing = self-destruction. Self-respect = self-enrichment.
- Homosexuality—as the American Psychiatric Association declared in 1973—is not a disease. Homophobia is a disease, like alcoholism or drug abuse.

- Homophobia, which is contagious, has been passed down to me. The self-loathing I am experiencing is merely a symptom of the disease of homophobia.
- I am not alone. All gay people experience self-loathing.
- Conditions "out there" don't have to change in order for me to stop feeling a sense of powerlessness or hopelessness; what I must do to end that feeling is to battle the self-loathing deep inside of me.
- I can love those who are afflicted with homophobia and understand that they are not intentionally meaning to hurt me, but I must not let them harm me or affect my emotional well-being. I must reject all of their hatred toward homosexuals and understand that their hatred is their disease talking, even when those speaking are my teachers, my religious leaders, and my own family.
- Self-loathing is so insidious that it affects all of my thinking about homosexuality and the gay community. All of the negative feelings I have toward gay people in general or certain types of gay people are a product of my own self-loathing.
- I will battle self-loathing all of my life and never fully be able to eradicate it. But I will be on guard to recognize it and to stop myself from behaving self-destructively, or acting in a homophobic manner toward other gay people.
- I will try every day of my life to deprogram myself, to love the gay man or lesbian that I am, and to replace my self-loathing with self-respect.

EXERCISE 4: WISHFUL THINKING

Go back to the piece of paper you folded up and put inside of this book. In the third column, the one that is blank, write a word that represents what you wish gay people were, what you hope gay people are, or what you would like them to be. For example: "smart," "fun," "exciting," "spiritual," etc. Your paper should then look something like this:

I am gay	faggot	smart
I am gay	freak	fun
I am gay	pansy	exciting
I am gay	pervert	spiritual

Keep filling in words until you have gone down the entire page.

Fold up the piece of paper and put it back inside this book; you will be coming back to it again. Now it is time to go on to Step 3 of the Outing Yourself process.

STEP 3

LEARNING THE TRUTH ABOUT BEING GAY

The number one way that society keeps gay people in the closet—and keeps gay people steeped in self-loathing—is by denying us our history and perpetuating myths about homosexuals. Learning about gay history, culture, and heritage, especially learning about the many influential lesbians and gay men who have gone before you, is crucial to helping you combat self-loathing and build self-esteem.

"I thought I had known what being a lesbian was all about," recalls Ann, a thirty-two-year-old architect who lives in a town in Ohio.

But it wasn't until I began reading about the lesbian and gay community that I had a true picture. It was as if someone took my blinders off. I had so many bad ideas about myself and about homosexuality. I believed a lot of myths and stereotypes, and I realized, after doing a lot of research, how much damage they had done. It was shocking in a way because I'm the kind of person who is usually really in touch and on top of things. I

was amazed that I could be duped in that way. But
that's how powerful homophobia is.

DOING RESEARCH

Step 3 requires you to do perhaps the most important
research of your entire life. More than any research
you've done before, this is all about learning about *you*. It
is about battling bad thoughts, shoring up your self-
esteem, and allowing the real you to come out.

You will have to go to the library and check out some
books—you may have to make a few trips. If you can
afford it, you might want to purchase some of the books
at a gay-positive bookstore, because they might be helpful
for future reference and as volumes you will cherish.

Becoming informed about lesbian and gay realities is a
step you will have to navigate according to the dictates of
your particular situation. If, for example, you are a
teenager living with your parents, you may feel there is
no way for you to bring the books home, for fear of their
being found. You may have to go to the library on a reg-
ular basis and read as much as you can in each sitting. If
you do bring the books home and you live with your parents, be sure that you do not "accidentally on purpose"
leave the books—or this book—out where your parents
can see them. The same is true about leaving the books
around at school or at the office. Perhaps you can check
one book out at a time, and always keep it in your book
bag.

Whatever the situation, you must be responsible for
making sure that others don't find your materials until
you are ready to confront them or be confronted by them.
Remember: One day you will not have to hide things such
as books or magazines; you are safeguarding yourself now
only to ease your coming-out process.

PLANNING A TRIP

Not every library or bookstore will have all the books listed in this chapter; some might not have any, particularly if you live in a small town. Understandably, if the town is small enough that you know the librarian, you may be afraid to inquire about the books. If any of these concerns pertain to you, plan a trip to a bigger city at some time in the future so that you can obtain the appropriate information. A trip is also a good idea because it will give you a sense of embarking on an adventure, looking for experiences that are exciting and new. Don't rush it, and make sure you plan so that you have enough time to explore at your leisure.

Depending on whether or not you can check the books out or bring them home, you may have to plan several trips. Even if you live in a big city, you may find that it's hard for you to read a lot in one sitting at the library. If you've checked the books out, you might not have much time to read. Give yourself room to breathe during this step. You are doing hard work that will benefit you in the long run. You are going to be taking in a lot of information, and the information needs to sink in and be processed. Everyone has a different timetable when it comes to this kind of work; however speedy a reader you are, this kind of life-altering reading will require a great deal of reflection. The important thing is for you to be relaxed and to go at your own pace. If you feel any anxiety about being found out, modify the way you are going about this step and let it take a longer time.

Uncovering the facts of gay life should be an enjoyable, interesting process. You will learn about yourself and the history of many people like you, about an entire culture that has been denied you. Sometimes all this information might be overwhelming, and you might feel sad or depressed. That response is normal, and it stems from the fact that you are realizing just how lost you have been all these years. Those feelings of sadness will eventually subside.

REMEMBER: CHECK FOR SELF-LOATHING

You will no doubt also find your self-loathing at work as you read and discover. You may still have hostile or negative feelings toward lesbians and gay men, and you might still react negatively to what you are reading. This too is normal; you should recognize it, understand it, and realize that you won't always react this way. In between readings, you might want to go back to the Meditation Notes several times to help you combat your self-loathing during this step.

BOOK LIST

These two books are collections of historical documents that show the history of lesbians and gay men in America:

Katz, Jonathan Ned. *Gay American History*. Revised ed. New York: Meridian, 1992.

Nestle, Joan. *The Persistent Desire: A Femme-Butch Reader*. Boston: Alyson Publications, 1992.

These three books give great answers to the most commonly asked questions about gay people:

Marcus, Eric. *Is It a Choice? Answers to 300 of the Most Frequently Asked Questions About Gays and Lesbians*. New York: HarperCollins, 1994.

Helminiak, Daniel A., Ph.D. *What the Bible Really Says About Homosexuality*. San Francisco: Alamo Square Press, 1994.

Berzon, Betty. *Setting Them Straight: A Guided Response to Antigay and Lesbian Bigotry.* New York: E. P. Dutton, 1995.

These two books tell the stories of some lesbians and gay men who went before us, some heroic, some not:
Duberman, Martin. *Stonewall.* New York: Plume, 1994.
Faderman, Lillian. *Odd Girls and Twilight Lovers: A History of Lesbian Life in the Twentieth Century.* New York: Penguin, 1992.

This controversial book lists 100 significant gay men and lesbians throughout history, some gay, some bi, some out, some outed:
Russell, Paul. *The Gay 100: A Ranking of the Most Important Gay Men and Lesbians, Past and Present.* New York: Citadel Press, 1995.

Because Acquired Immune Deficiency Syndrome—AIDS—is such a risk to everyone, you should be sure to obtain the latest information on safer-sex practices that can protect people from HIV, the virus that causes AIDS. This is especially true if you have been sexually active, or plan to be. All AIDS-service organizations in major cities will send you safer-sex guidelines. If you don't know of one, call the National AIDS Hotline at 800-342-2437 and be sure to ask for the number of an AIDS service organization in your area that works primarily in the gay community. The following two books will also offer you safer-sex guidelines (take note that both books are sexually explicit):
Silverstein, Charles, Ph.D., and Felice Picano. *The New Joy of Gay Sex.* New York: HarperCollins, 1993.
Tatchell, Peter. *Safer Sexy: The Guide to Gay Sex Safely.* New York: Freedom Editions, 1994.

EXERCISE 5: WISH FULFILLMENT

After you have read about our gay heritage and our lesbian and gay lives today, go back to the piece of paper that you had folded up in this book.

Look across the page at the third column where you listed all of the positive things you'd hoped gay people would represent.

Now that you have done the reading, you have a fuller and much more real sense of who and what lesbians and gay men are. Go down the list and put a check-mark next to each word you had written if it fits with what you have read.

Do this process slowly, owning each word, and realizing how much of what you'd hoped gay men and lesbians were is true. By the end, you should have checked off most if not all of the words you'd written down.

Take a good look at the second column, reading the epithets about homosexuality and realizing how powerless they are to you now, how you don't even see them as negative any longer. You now own those words, not the people who've always hurled them at you, and neither the words nor the people can do you any harm.

Look down the list of positive words and see how they represent the truth about gay people. Think of the individual stories and anecdotes you have read about that apply to these words.

Connect those stories to the positive words on the page. For example, if you had written down the word "brave," you might want to apply it to the people who stood up to the police at the Stonewall Inn riots or the women who emerged from the military and came out of the closet as lesbians after World War II. Commit yourself to spreading the truth about gay people—the truth you've read about—

and use these words you've connected to the stories to describe gay people whenever you talk about them.

FEELING PROUD

Put this piece of paper back in the book now, and at any time in the future during the Outing Yourself process, when you feel self-loathing rearing its ugly head, return to this paper, read the positive words, and think about the stories you've attached to them. Along with the Meditation Notes in Step 2, this piece of paper will be a source of strength and inspiration every time you need it.

Part I of the Outing Yourself process is now complete, and you should be very proud of yourself. You have made the first steps toward coming out of the closet and you should take a break here and reward yourself. Buy yourself something nice, perhaps a favorite food, a new piece of clothing, or something for your home, your apartment, your bedroom, or your workstation. Celebrate by starting a journal. Whatever you do, make sure it is something positive that you can associate with the positive experience of having made the first steps toward coming out.

It is important at this point to reflect on what you've done and reward yourself: You deserve to feel a sense of accomplishment and to take a breather so that you will be rested and prepared for the hard work ahead.

After fully completing Step 3, you should begin to notice a change in yourself: You should feel a bit better about who you are. You have become well-informed about gay issues and more confident thinking and talking about them. And you are prepared to move on to Part

II in the Outing Yourself process: Outing Yourself to
Other Gay People.

You may feel both excitement and some anxiety, perhaps even fear. That's normal. You will know it is time
to move on when your excitement outweighs the anxiety
and fear—when in spite of whatever fears you may have,
you are bursting to explore this new world you've read
about.

PART II

OUTING YOURSELF
to OTHER GAY PEOPLE

MEETING OTHER GAY PEOPLE

When they search out other gay people as friends and companions, the first place most gay people think about—and indeed, for decades the only place that gay people were able to meet—is the gay or lesbian bar.

"The gay bar was then, and continued to be for a long time, the place where a real community gathered," wrote author Michael Bronski of the late 1960s, when he was first stepping out of the closet. "In those days there were no gay newspapers, no newsletters, no gay media of any kind. The bars were not just places to drink, they were our community centers, our town squares, our back fences that we could hang over and gossip, our local bulletin boards."

Today, however, the gay community has newspapers, community centers, bulletin boards, and, in some cities, even town squares. Gay bars today are more likely to be places for people to drink and have a good time with friends and look for love, just as straight bars are. While you can meet some very nice people in bars, they might

not be the best places for long discussions or making last-
ing friendships. Bars will certainly not provide you with
the broad perspective on gay life that your coming-out
process requires. And if you are under twenty-one, bars
are not an option for you at all in most states.

"I met some of my best friends in local bars," says Jerry,
a twenty-eight-year-old accountant who lives in Seattle.

> But in general I found the bar scene very shallow. I'd
> say I met most of my friends through community orga-
> nizations and support groups. I met more people of dif-
> ferent ages in the community groups, because bars tend
> to attract only people of the particular age group that
> the bar caters to, and bars also tend to split along racial
> lines. All of my friends who are black or Asian I met
> while doing volunteer work through gay community
> organizations or AIDS service groups.
>
> And bars are also split along gender lines, too. I have
> a lot of lesbian friends, but I didn't meet any of them
> in bars. One of my closest friends, Olivia, I met at a
> coming-out support group. I met another close friend,
> Christine, soon after that, when I got involved in a gay
> political organization. They were really my first close
> friends. Eventually I had a network of friends.

As Jerry emphasizes, bars should not be the only—or
even the first—place you go to in order to meet other gay
people and come out to them. In larger urban areas there
are churches, schools, and gay community centers where
many different kinds of gay groups regularly meet—from
gay and lesbian high school student groups to gay and lesbian doctors and lawyers groups to gay and lesbian political groups (Democrat and Republican) to gay and lesbian
Catholic, Protestant, and Jewish groups. There are support groups and even "orientation" meetings that help

people deal with coming out. As Jerry noted, gay and AIDS organizations in which you can volunteer your time will also put you in contact with many different types of gay people. These are the perfect arenas for meeting others who are at the same stage of the process that you are, as well as people farther along who can offer you help.

MORE RESEARCH

There are several directories that provide extensive listings of gay and lesbian community organizations. *Gayellow Pages: The National Edition* has served the community for over twenty years (there are also more specific New York/New Jersey, Northeast, and South/South Midwest editions). For a great many people, this book has been indispensable in their coming-out process.

Gayellow Pages offers a state-by-state, city-by-city listing of lesbian and gay organizations, community centers, publications, businesses, archives, college and university gay and lesbian groups, conferences, and many other establishments and institutions that serve the gay, lesbian, and bisexual communities. If you cannot find a copy of *Gayellow Pages* locally, you may write to Renaissance House, P.O. Box 533, Village Station, New York, NY 10014 or call (212) 674-0120 to find out how to receive a copy mailed in a sealed, unmarked envelope.

COMING-OUT SUPPORT GROUPS

Another way to find places for you to meet other gay, lesbian, or bisexual people is to check your local yellow pages and white pages for lesbian and gay community centers or any gay and lesbian political or support groups.

When and if you do find a gay community center or any other kind of gay group that is near to you, call up and ask someone there when the coming-out support groups meet. Nearly every center has some version of such a group.

"I really needed to be in a coming-out support group, not so much to learn about coming out but to meet people who were going through it too," recalls Kate, a thirty-three-year-old Hartford, Connecticut, boutique owner.

> I already had my basic plan for coming out and it wasn't like I wanted more tips or more ideas. I just needed to know there was support, that there were other women and men going through it. Basically, I didn't have any lesbian friends at the time and didn't know any gay men, and it was a place where I could meet new people but not feel embarrassed because I was still closeted.

COLLEGES AND UNIVERSITIES

If there is not a gay community center or gay group near you, check with some of the colleges and universities in your area. Many have lesbian and gay support groups or gay campus political organizations. Gay student leaders will not only often be helpful in directing you to on-campus coming-out support groups in which you might be able to participate, but they will also be able to direct you to groups that meet in your area that are not affiliated with the university and are open to all.

"I think the people at the university saved my life," says Frances, a thirty-year-old housekeeper who lives in a small town in western Massachusetts.

> I was feeling so sad and lonely, knowing I was a lesbian but not knowing who to turn to. I often wanted to die—really, just die. I don't have much family—none, really. My father left home when I was young and my

mother and I don't talk any longer; she was hooked on drugs for a while, and I left when I was old enough to get out on my own. That was in Dallas.

I moved away and lived with my aunt for a while in Houston, working and saving my money, and then I left and came up north six years ago. Soon after I moved here, I saw something on a wall when I was over by the university about a gay dance and saw the phone number of the group that was sponsoring it. I called them up and said I thought I might be homosexual but that I'd never met anyone who was gay and needed to talk.

These women were just wonderful; they had me come in and sit with them for hours, just talking about what lesbian life was like, and they gave me some books and information. I met a lot of gay men there too over the next few weeks. It changed my whole outlook on gays and lesbians, and I felt so much better about myself. I really no longer have the sad thoughts I used to have, because I finally reached out to people.

SMALL-TOWN AND RURAL AMERICA

Of course, gay centers and groups often exist only in big cities or in towns where there are colleges and universities. Roger is a twenty-one-year-old retail clerk who lives in a small town in Tennessee, a two-hour drive from any college, university, or city, let alone a gay establishment of any kind.

I feel so alone. I wouldn't even think about asking any of my friends if they know anyone gay who I could talk to. My only connection with gay life has been through reading about it, sneaking books out of the library. I've written letters to gay authors, but that's the only contact I've ever made with gays. I didn't know of any gay bars or social groups or gay organizations or anything like that until very recently, but it doesn't matter because they're all too far away. I'm feeling that there are no gay people around here for miles and miles and miles. Or if there are, I think it's impossible for me to find them.

Roger speaks for many people who, thanks to books, magazines, and (increasingly) television, are learning more about themselves from other gay people but who are not able to communicate with them. Yet gay people are everywhere, even in most rural areas, and they can and do find one another.

Contrary to what Roger might think, he is not alone. Many gay men and lesbians, though they may be much more circumspect than their big-city counterparts, meet, socialize, and assist one another in small-town and rural America. Often, even in the most remote places, there is a newspaper or magazine that runs personal ads and pen-pal ads for gay people looking for friendship—or there is a publication from a nearby big city that includes readers in outlying areas. If you live in a remote place, call a gay group or community center in the nearest big city—no matter how far away it is—and ask about gay publications and gay groups that serve your local community. Some national organizations, such as Parents, Families, and Friends of Lesbians and Gays (P-Flag), which is based in Washington but has chapters throughout the country, can be very helpful. P-Flag's Washington office—(202) 638-4200—will direct you to a local P-Flag chapter that may be able to assist you in meeting gay people in your area. They will also provide you with information you'll find useful later when speaking to your parents about being gay.

Wayne is a seventeen-year-old high school student who

lives in a small town in Georgia. He has not yet told his parents that he is gay—though he says he plans to as soon as he is finished with school.

> I really do feel plugged in with the gay community, even though you might say I'm isolated. I read gay magazines and newspapers that I have been able to get through the mail, and so I have learned much about the gay community, both nationally and locally—and that's real funny because before I didn't think there even *was* a local gay community.
>
> I called P-Flag and received much more information, plus a lot of moral support. I called there several times, just to talk. They sent me some information for gay youth, and in one of the publications they sent me I found a gay pen-pal in an advertisement. We began writing each other, first every couple of weeks, then, like, twice a week. We finally met—he lived four hours away. We met in between, each of us taking the bus two hours. It was great finally meeting this person who I really felt I knew so well; I would say he was my best friend, even though I'd never met him. The next time we got together, he brought another friend, and we exchanged addresses and have gotten together a couple of times. I now have eight gay male pen pals, and one lesbian pen pal. I really consider all of them my best friends.

BE SPECIFIC ABOUT YOUR NEEDS

When you call any group for information and assistance, try to be specific about your situation. While it's important that you eventually meet gay people from all walks of life, at first you might be more comfortable with gay people who have a lot in common with you. If you are a lesbian, gay, or bisexual teenager, when you call community groups be sure to tell them you're a teen so that they can direct you to gay youth groups. If you are black, Hispanic, Asian, or part of any other ethnic minority, you might want to let them know so that they can suggest groups that provide services to gay people of specific ethnic groups. If you are religious, ask about gay religious groups in your area and mention your religion and denomination specifically. If you are seeking a new denomination because your current congregation's tone is antigay, you might want to also ask about gay-friendly houses of worship. If you are a Christian lesbian or gay man, you might want to inquire about the gay-founded Metropolitan Community Church and ask if there is one near you. If you live in an isolated area, ask about pen pals and other services that might be available to you so that you can communicate with people outside of your area.

GETTING ON-LINE

Perhaps the newest and fastest-growing way gay, lesbian, and bisexual people are meeting these days is "on-line," via computers. Tens of thousands of gay people, many of whom live in rural areas, communicate with one another daily without seeing one another or even speaking with one another orally, exchanging information as they make their first tentative steps out of the closet.

Put simply, being on-line means that your computer is connected, via your telephone line, to a network of hundreds of thousands, perhaps millions, of other computers. Your keyboard allows you to communicate with anyone else who is on-line. People who go on-line often come together to speak about many different topics in community forums, or "rooms," where anyone can participate in the live conversation at hand simply by typing in their thoughts and ideas. Another way that people have discussions and exchange information on-line is via "bulletin boards" on which people post messages about specific topics and respond to previous postings.

While people from all walks of life are today using on-line services, this new form of communication has been particularly useful for lesbian, gay, and bisexual people who are struggling with the closet. For the first time they can access information and talk to other gay people without meeting face to face, without stepping into a gay bar or other gay establishment, and without even speaking to a person on the telephone. And they can remain completely anonymous. Most people on-line in fact do not use their real names, instead adopting interesting "screen names."

Certainly, on-line services have been instrumental in helping to disseminate information to people who are still so fearful that they won't go to a gay group or call one on the telephone. But they have also been immensely important for people who are farther along in coming out but who simply live far away from any gay group or other gay establishment. For people in such isolated places, on-line services have been a godsend.

"I couldn't imagine what my life would be like if I wasn't on-line," says Philip, a twenty-seven-year-old real estate agent who lives in his native rural Pennsylvania.

> Quite honestly, I think I would not be gay—or rather, I would not be out of the closet. I'd still be a tormented closet case. I would see living a gay life as an option that was completely unavailable to me. I was dating women all these years and not being fulfilled. I guess deep down I knew I wanted to be with men but I just ignored it—or tried to. All of that made me miserable; I hated life, but I wouldn't admit to myself why.
>
> Soon after our office got on-line, I discovered a gay

bulletin board. I'd wait until everyone left the office and go on-line. I started having discussions with people who were gay who lived right in the area as well as people who live all across the country. It was so provocative for me to explore it, so exciting—but also very safe. I didn't feel I was losing control or that anyone could figure out who I was.

I could communicate with these people and use a name that I thought suited me, like Niceguy—that was the first name I used—and have great discussions, and then at any time I could bow out. Eventually, I began talking with some of these people on the telephone, and then I actually began meeting them. Now I'm in a relationship with someone—only a year after first going on-line. I swear, I don't think I would have known any gay men at all had it not been for this system. I think I'd still be living a straight life and hating it. I wouldn't have even known there were any gay people around here.

Lesbians and gay men in larger cities have also found on-line services valuable, particularly teenagers and others who cannot yet fully explore gay life, even when it may exist right in their own backyards.

"When I found this world on-line it was like discovering a buried treasure," says sixteen-year-old Reed, a high school student who lives in Brooklyn, New York.

I've known I was gay since I was little, maybe five or six, but I couldn't just tell my parents about it. I thought I'd wait until I could live on my own so I could *be* gay first, and then tell my parents. And I thought that wouldn't be until I was, like, twenty. At my age it doesn't matter much to me that the gay capital of the planet is right over the bridge in Manhattan. For me it may as well be a million miles away. I'm not allowed in Manhattan unless I have to do a school project.

But I told my parents a lot sooner than I thought—that's because of being on-line. My parents had bought me this computer last year and a modem and put me on America Online [an on-line service]. My father was on AOL at work and he said it would be educational. Boy, it was *really* educational! I found the Gay and Lesbian Forum and downloaded tons of information. Then I was having conversations with all of these other kids my age who were gay or lesbian or bisexual or just, you know, confused. Once in a while straight kids come in to talk too. Now I have a whole new group of friends and I don't hang out with my old friends anymore, because they're homophobic. I talk with my new friends about everything. I talk about boys I have crushes on, and about how I came out to my parents—I'm like the role model now for that, because it went so well, and now everyone wishes they could do it. So now everybody on-line is coming out to their parents because I did.

There are many different on-line services available that serve the gay community, and Gayellow Pages lists several of them. America Online, the service Reed subscribes to, has a Gay and Lesbian Forum in which a person can access information from and about all of the national lesbian and gay organizations, such as the Gay and Lesbian Alliance Against Defamation (GLAAD) and Parents, Family, and Friends of Lesbians and Gays (P-Flag). On any given day there are hundreds of discussions occurring live on America Online's Gay and Lesbian Forum about political as well as personal issues affecting gay men and women, and there are also gay bulletin boards servicing teens, African-Americans, Latinos, Jews, Italians, twentysomethings, thirtysomethings, fortysomethings, transgendered people, bisexuals, journalists, authors, teachers, and just about everyone else.

"The fact that I could go on AOL and find other lesbians who were sexually abused and sexually harassed because they were lesbians makes AOL one of the most important tools for supporting people within this community," says Shirley, a thirty-five-year-old teacher who lives on New York's Long Island.

> After what I'd gone through, being sexually abused as a child and then later as an adult, and knowing that in my case it was all tied to homophobia because I was being abused by men who were trying to make me "straight," I needed support, and yet I was so closeted I refused to go to any support groups and expose myself. On AOL, I found that support. On bulletin boards I found so many other lesbians who'd been through this experience. Eventually, just being able to talk to people helped me to deal with my closet. Slowly, I came out, after meeting so many other lesbians who had a similar experience.

There are many other on-line services, such as CompuServe and Prodigy, and the Internet, each of which provides varying levels of service to the gay community. Of course, on-line services are not economically feasible for everyone; computers are costly, and there are also fees for subscribing to on-line services. However, as the price of computers continues to drop, along with fees for on-line services, more and more people will have access to computers; in the future, every household may well possess a computer, with much of our daily work, from banking to shopping, done on-line.

For now, if you don't have a computer already and can't afford one, perhaps you can get access to a computer and on-line services through schools, libraries, and universities in your area. This technology is continuing to revolutionize lesbian and gay life, not only for closeted people who find each other but also for those who have already come out. It might be worth your while to talk to computer professionals about a cost-efficient way you can purchase a computer and have access to on-line services, so you too can be a part of the gay future on-line.

MOVING TO FORM BONDS

Once your research into gay life evolves into contact with flesh-and-blood gay people, you will have moved past stereotype into a warmer, if more complex, reality. You'll feel more comfortable with other gay people, and thus a bit more comfortable with yourself. You'll see that you have something powerful in common with other gay people, even though you may all be very different. You'll realize that your common ground is so broad that you will be able to bond and create profound friendships with some of the people you've met. When you come to this realization—and for some people this will happen after they've met only a few gay people, while for others it will happen only after they have met many—you'll know that it is time to move on to Step 5 in the Outing Yourself process.

STEP 5

DEVELOPING A FAMILY OF FRIENDS

When you finally do meet other gay people, coming out to them will not be a major task. Just by reaching out to them, you are already coming out. Whenever you develop a bond of friendship—even if it begins as a sexual attraction—it can be the beginning of a network of friends. New friends usually introduce you to *their* friends, who in turn often become still more new friends. In general, perhaps because they have often been isolated for so long, gay people seem to make friends quickly and bond closely.

A family of friends is important because we lesbian and gay people are often alienated from our biological families. Because we were not brought up as gay, because we were forced to hide and to live as heterosexuals, we were denied a family life in which we could grow and prosper as our true selves. In many ways we have a lot of catching up to do. We also need to feel accepted by people like ourselves because homosexuality is so detested in the larger world; being around people similar to ourselves, who love us and support us, helps build self-respect and battle self-loathing—both of which, as you have already learned, are fundamental to coming out.

Even if you are already dating someone of the same sex or getting involved with someone in a sexual relationship, it is still essential that you develop this family of gay friends to aid your coming-out process. It is natural to feel more confident and more proud if and when you are in love, but a network of friends is important when romance wanes or causes trauma, pain, or isolation. Before going on to the often demanding task of confiding in the straight people in your life, you will need gay people close to you, people who will always be there, no matter what, and who understand what you are going through without judgment and condescension.

"My gay and lesbian friends have been like my life-support system," says Alex, a twenty-one-year-old college student in Phoenix, Arizona.

It has really been, well, exciting—exciting finding out about my sexuality. And my friends have been a big part of that. I met my friend John in one of my classes when I was a freshman. We both knew—that "gaydar" thing—and we bonded quickly and confided in each other. Then the both of us went to the lesbian and gay group on campus and met more people, and a bunch of us became close.

Some people had other friends they'd met at bars or in activist groups, and they also became part of our group. What's great is that it's a mixed group; I find that my lesbian friends, as women, have a different perspective on coming out that's really helpful. As women, they've been more clued in for a longer amount of time about prejudice and living with a certain amount of fear and needing to just bust loose.

A NETWORK

While some gay men and lesbians may have a family of friends that is quite small—maybe as few as three people—others, like Alex, have a particularly large group. But the size of the group doesn't seem to inhibit the ability of the people in it to become tightly knit, as Alex himself discovered.

> I'd say my group of friends is now like fifteen or twenty people. We're really close, really solid. I think any of us would do anything for each other. I've helped John through a couple of tough spots, like when over one summer his mother found some letters he'd gotten from his boyfriend. He had been planning on coming out to his mother and father just before he went back to school, so that they'd have that time apart to think about it and let it sink in. But she found the letters in June, while he had to spend the next two months there. I must have been on the telephone with him twice a day for two weeks; he was very upset—and needless to say, so were they. Neither of us had any money, you know, being college students on summer break, but by literally counting our pennies and borrowing money from some of our other friends, we got him a plane ticket so he could come back to Phoenix [from California] for a couple of weeks to chill out. It was exactly what he needed, a sort of refueling of support, so that he could go back and face the music. Eventually things worked out, but I don't know what he'd have done without that support.

Alex describes the family of friends in a way that sounds like a true family.

> Everyone's got their own problems, and sometimes there's tension—I mean, it can be as dysfunctional as

your biological family. But people care in that certain way where they put others before them. Most of my friends are going through coming out themselves. They're roughly the same age as I am and they're experiencing gay life for the first time. I think you really need to relate to people who are going through exactly what you are. At the same time, I have a couple of older friends in our crowd, guys who have been out for a long, long time, and they're just as important to me. They give me a lot of advice that is valuable because they've been through a lot of this before.

DON'T RUSH

Developing a family of friends is not something you accomplish over one happy weekend. It takes time to develop friendships and bonds with people. For some people this process will take weeks or months; for others it may take years.

"My first relationship with a woman began when I was twenty-one," says Judy, a twenty-eight-year-old graphic designer who lives in New York City.

But it wasn't until this year that I can actually say I have what you might call a family of friends. For a while, the woman I was involved with was the only lesbian friend I had. She helped me out a lot, especially in dealing with my family, but I would say that developing other bonds, particularly when we broke up, was essential.

In terms of coming out, I don't think I could have gone any further without a bigger support net. I had come out to some straight friends and to my brother, but I didn't come out to my parents until this year, and I don't think I'd have been able to do that without the input from my friends. They don't all know each other, and they range in age from about twenty-three to about fifty. Most are lesbians but one close friend is a gay man. They've all been so important, in so many different ways. Some of them are just like *there*, you know? They don't say anything really, because sometimes there's nothing to say. You turn to them when you just need someone to lean on or listen to you. Others don't stop talking—they're the ones that always have something to say, some piece of wisdom, some sound advice. You really need both—and more.

PEOPLE YOU CAN TRUST

As Judy points out, while your network of friends may be like your true family in terms of the strong bonds you have with its members, your family of friends doesn't have to be a family in the traditional sense, where you all know one another intimately and live together or assemble on holidays. In fact, none of your friends need to know the others at all. What is important is that each of your friends knows *you* intimately. It's important that you have several people you can talk to and trust and whose advice you respect.

"It must have been about three years before I felt comfortable enough with my new friends and knew they'd be there for me," says Carla, an actress who lives in Los Angeles. Now thirty-four, Carla was closeted throughout her twenties, but recently she came out to two heterosexual friends, women who were her closest confidantes in college. She is now gearing up to tell her family.

I needed my [lesbian] friends [in order to come out] and I guess it needed to take that long to develop friends. But everyone is different. It took me three years to make friends, and it also took me about ten years to even admit to myself that I was gay after first thinking I was, when I was twenty. But my friend Kathy was like Speedy Gonzales at this. We became friends just six months ago, when she first came out. She's twenty-four. I was the second lesbian she met, and she then became close with me and three of my other friends. Within three months she felt tight enough with us and strong enough to tell some of her straight friends that she's gay. And last week she told her mother! At first I was kind of embarrassed. I mean, she makes me look like a snail at this. But then I thought, Well, I'm slow at everything. I guess everybody's got to go at their own pace.

ALL FAMILIES OF FRIENDS ARE DIFFERENT

Like Carla, it may be a while before you are secure enough and comfortable enough with your lesbian and gay friends to move on to telling the straight people in your life that you are gay. Or you may be like Carla's friend Kathy and feel you have that support group within only a few months of becoming friends with gay people. Your family of friends may be made up of more than twenty people, like Alex's, or it might be as small as three or four. Like Alex's friends, all of your friends might know one another, or like Judy's, they may not. You may find that your family of friends is made up of both men and women, or you may find that it is made up of people only of your own sex.

Your family of friends will be unique to you and not exactly like anyone else's; there are no hard-and-fast rules as to what makes up a family of friends or how long that network will take to assemble. You will know when you have a family of friends and when their support encourages you to move on in the Outing Yourself process. You will be filled with confidence as a gay person, and you will feel so good about your new friends that you'll want very much to share those feelings with others in your life.

You'll know that you're ready to progress when, for what might be the first time in your life, you feel happy about being gay.

PART III

OUTING YOURSELF TO YOUR STRAIGHT FRIENDS

TELLING YOUR BEST FRIEND

Coming out to the first straight person in your life is cause for anxiety, but it can also be liberating and exciting. That may be especially true if you're coming out to your best straight friend.

"I'll never forget that kind of kinetic charge I got when I told my best friend, Susan," recalls Allison, a fifty-three-year-old former schoolteacher who lives in Albany, New York.

I must have been about thirty, living in Philadelphia, where I was born and raised. Susan was about to get married to a man, and I was involved secretly with a woman, Helen, whom I had introduced to Susan as my "friend" from my cooking class, which met two nights a week. There really was no cooking class, of course—I just made that up so I wouldn't have to explain where I was on those nights and so I could explain where my new "friend" came from.

In those days [1971], this kind of thing was quite

shocking. But I was feeling so marvelous at the time, completely walking on air, really just wonderful—and quite unstoppable. I was in love at the time with Helen, a woman I stayed with for twelve years, and I had some wonderful, wonderful lesbian friends, some of whom are still with me. I guess I would have been disappointed if Susan didn't take it well, but I can't say it would have killed me. This was about me and who I was, and if Susan couldn't take it, it would have been sad for a moment but I'd get over it. I'd just go lead my life with my lesbian friends—they certainly had more than enough love to go around. I expected that Susan would take it well, though; we were both open-minded kind of people. Just gearing up to tell her gave me a charge. I felt I could finally share something about myself with her that I'd kept secret.

I took her to our favorite restaurant, and told her I was taking her out to dinner because I wanted to celebrate something—that I had something to tell her about my life that was exciting. Then, during our first course, after a nice glass of red wine, I told her that since she was getting married, and becoming intimate with someone, she needed to know that I too was very intimate with someone in the same way—but that it wasn't a man.

Allison had decided that a good way to reveal that she was a lesbian was by telling Susan that her "friend" Helen was more than just a friend, and thus letting Susan know that she too was in love. Allison wanted to make sure this news was not perceived as an admission of something bad; she would make it clear to Susan that this news made her proud and happy.

I said it was something I'd struggled with for quite some time but that now I was feeling good about it, and that I wasn't telling her in order to gain her sympathy or even moral support but rather because I wanted to share how marvelous I felt and that I couldn't continue being friends with her and living a lie. She seemed a bit stunned at first; you know, she had that kind of blank look that straight people sometimes get when you reveal yourself to them. But then, after asking a lot of questions, she got used to it rather quickly—before dessert—and she told me she was honored that I had told her, that it made her feel closer to me. I felt the same way toward her, and really very proud of myself too.

MAKING THIS ONE EASY

Having made some gay friends and been honest with them, as Allison did, you should be feeling good enough about being gay that you are probably bursting to tell your straight friends. You might think of first telling your best friend, the person with whom you most share confidences and the one you think would be the most understanding. This first disclosure will be like a practice run for your later disclosures to your other friends and your family. Try to make this one an easy one; later on you can take on those friends you know or suspect to be rigid, insensitive, or antigay. If the person you are thinking of telling is not someone you feel will accept you unconditionally, think about telling someone else first. Talk it over with your gay friends; remember, you are no longer alone. You now have at your side a supportive chosen family, most of whom have gone through this kind of encounter themselves. By listening and offering advice, they can be very helpful in assessing whether the heterosexual friend you are thinking about is the right one for you to come out to first.

It's also important to talk with gay friends to make sure that your own self-loathing is not at work. You may be telling yourself that certain straight individuals in your life—or even all of them—will never understand you when in fact they might be the very people who would understand the most. Because of the fear and anxiety associated with coming out, self-loathing often plays tricks on us and tells us things are impossible when they are not. Your gay friends will be able to help you sort things out and assess situations more accurately.

The first heterosexual person you tell could be anyone in your life: For some people, that first straight person is a close friend; for others, it is simply a friend who is understanding and willing to listen. If you are a teenager, you might choose someone your age who is quite grown-up about these issues, or you might decide that friends your own age are not mature enough to handle this information. You might want to talk to someone who is a little bit older. In some cases, an understanding cousin, sister, or brother might be the person, but often, if you're going to talk openly, you will want to stay out of the biological family circle for a while. If you feel strongly that a sibling is truly the first straight person you'd like to come out to—or if you are still unsure—you might want to jump ahead and read the section "Telling Other Family Members" in Step 8 (pages 85–88), and then come back here to proceed with this step.

STAY IN CONTROL

In any case, you must confide in only the most caring and accepting person you know. Trustworthiness is important, because this person will have to keep your news private for at least a while. It is important that you keep control over your coming-out process. Someday you won't care who talks about your sexuality, but right now keeping a sense of your own power is paramount. Control over this information about yourself is part of the mastery you maintain over your own life.

"I was nineteen, and I had made a lot of gay friends," says Peter, a Seattle student who is now twenty-one, about the gay youth center he used to frequent.

> I used to go there after school, for maybe a little over a year, and no one knew about me but the people there, who were all lesbians and gay guys. I wanted to break out of that and tell someone, anyone, outside of gay people just to at least see what the reaction would be. I guess I was getting restless and wanted to try it out, as a way of building up to telling my family. Doing everything undercover is a little bit fun at first, but after a while you feel like a real freak. I was tired of it.
>
> I was thinking about talking to some of my [straight] friends who were my age but I was too afraid of how they might react; every time I thought they could handle it, somebody would throw around the word "faggot" to describe somebody they saw, and everybody would laugh. And that would tell me it wasn't a good idea just yet.
>
> I eventually decided to talk to a friend of the family, a woman who my parents were close with. She was older than me but younger than my parents—she used to be my mom's assistant at work ten years ago, and she even had baby-sat for me and my sister a couple of times. When she stopped working for my mom, she kept in touch and visited a lot and came for the holidays.
>
> Karen was almost like part of the family—her own family lived on the East Coast, so she didn't get to see them much—and my father and my sisters liked her a lot. I knew I could tell Karen because she was never

judgmental toward me or anyone and always seemed willing to listen to people, and I always sensed that she knew about me anyway.

It turns out she did think I was gay, and she was glad I spoke to her about it. She has gay friends and knew a lot about the gay community. I eventually told her boyfriend, Jim, so I guess he was the second straight person I came out to. I was glad to finally speak to people who weren't gay but who were okay about it and who knew my family.

I still am building up to coming out to my mom and dad and my sisters. It's something I really want to do, but I'm afraid. I keep going back and forth on it. Every time I get up the nerve to do it, I chicken out. My gay friends totally understand what I'm going through. But Karen and Jim are great too, because they're an example of how understanding straight people can be about this, and that inspires me and gives me, I guess, a bit of hope about my family and how they could react when I do talk to them.

Once you have decided which straight person you will come out to, it's important to sit back and evaluate the situation. Are any negative thoughts welling up inside of you? Not only do you want to keep yourself from backing down on your determination to come out, but you also don't want yourself to appear apologetic or self-diminishing. Self-loathing could sabotage you, impairing your judgment and undermining your courage and your self-esteem.

MAKING A MENTAL PICTURE

Exercise 6 will empower you to make the positive happen—but first, it is crucial to read the following passage just before each time you perform the exercise.

ENVISIONING

It is true that some things in my life are out of my control, but many things are very much within my power. Self-fulfilling prophecies occur when I consciously or unconsciously work to create a specific outcome. That outcome can be positive or negative. When it is negative it can be very destructive. I may consciously want positive results, but because I am afraid or guilt-ridden or—in this case—filled with inevitable and hidden self-loathing about being gay, a certain part of me will work against my efforts.

I must work to make sure this doesn't happen. Therefore:

I am determined *not* to envision that which is negative.

I am determined *not* to envision scenarios in which people react negatively to my homosexuality.

I am determined to envision only scenarios in which the people who are important to me react with concern, understanding, and care.

There is always the possibility that people will react negatively, and it is important to master ways to handle such situations and to cope with any related stress. But *being prepared for a possibility* is different from *envisioning* one. In the former case, we take certain precautions in order to protect ourselves; in the latter, we will it to be. For example, you may have thought about the possibility of a fire in your home and may have prepared for the possibility—keeping fire extinguishers on hand and knowing where fire exits are—but surely you don't sit around imagining yourself trapped in your home, overcome by smoke. *That* would be envisioning disaster. Even if these thoughts vaguely come into your mind once or twice, you are not obsessed about the possibility of a fire to the point where you are racked with fear.

And so, from now on, that is how you must treat the possibility of a negative reaction to your homosexuality: a serious and real possibility that you will be prepared for, but not something you will waste time obsessing about.

Instead, the next exercise will help you envision people reacting *positively* to your coming out. Any time a negative thought about coming out enters your mind, you can replace it by envisioning a positive outcome. You will have to be diligent and disciplined at this, making sure you do not obsess about the negative.

EXERCISE 6: ENVISIONING

Sit down in a comfortable place and think about coming out to the person you are planning to come out to.

Picture the place: a familiar setting that you both are comfortable in.

Envision yourself in a upbeat mood, not nervous, anxious, or sad. You are happy and content, and you are confiding in your friend because you want to share something about yourself that you feel good about.

Picture yourself saying, "There's something I want to tell you about myself. I want to share it because, although it took a lot of time to come to terms with it, I'm very comfortable and happy about it. I want to tell you because I trust you and because you're close to me. [Pause] I am a lesbian—I am gay."

Think about how that person might respond positively. What would a positive response be? What would he or she do? What questions would he or she have?

Create the scenario that describes the most positive outcome you can imagine. Write it down. Fill in as much detail
as possible. Where exactly are you meeting? What are you
wearing? What time of day is it? How much time will you
spend together? What will you do afterward?

Go over the scenario again and again until believing it
becomes second nature.

Let its positive feelings fill you deeply.

For the next few days, or however long it takes, go to a
quiet place a few times each day, and envision the scenario
again. During these days or weeks, whenever negative
thoughts about coming out rise up, whenever your mind
begins to construct a negative scenario, whenever you see
mental images of people reacting negatively or with hostility,
stop yourself and envision the positive. Put the negative
thoughts out of your mind by envisioning your positive scenario. This process requires diligence and perseverance.

You are, of course, trying to create a new and positive self-
fulfilling prophecy. Think about all the aspects of your created scenario that make it a positive one. Think about what
you can do to make it happen.

Think about what conditions in your envisioned scenario—the setting, the day, the time, your friend's mood,
your own mood—will need to be duplicated in real life in
order to have that positive outcome.

PLANNING AHEAD

After you have performed the envisioning exercise frequently over a period of time, and when you are finally
ready to come out to a straight friend, there are a few
more things you must do.

First, make sure you give yourself and your friend

enough time to talk at length; don't plan your coming
out to be rushed. You will both need time to sit and
absorb how the other feels. Your friend may have a lot of
questions to ask—which you can answer, because you
have worked to inform yourself about the lesbian and
gay community, and because you have a circle of gay
friends.

Second, make sure that you have told one or more of
your gay friends about your plan, including when you
plan to proceed with it. One of your gay friends should
be available to talk with you after your encounter.

The setting in which you tell your friend is also
important. Allison's method of coming out—taking her
friend to dinner—is a great idea. You might want to do
the same—or go for coffee or ice cream. Make it a place
that isn't too crowded—so you can talk freely. Make
sure it is a happy, comfortable setting that both of you
will enjoy or perhaps have already enjoyed together in
the past.

When you are ready, talk to your friend in the way you
envisioned. Be sure to tell your friend that your being gay
is something you feel good about. Say that you are sharing
this information because you care about and trust your
friend and because you need to confide in someone. Then
proceed the way you envisioned.

Don't stammer, don't stutter, and, above all, don't back
down. Don't say anything to the effect of "I've got to tell
you something, but it's real hard" or "This is really upsetting."

Above all, do not be negative, vague, or evasive. It's
important that you do this in a way that is natural and
positive. It should not sound rehearsed or unlike you, but
it should clearly communicate the statement from the
envisioning exercise: "There's something I want to tell

you about myself. I want to share it because although it took time for me to come to terms with it, I'm very comfortable and happy about it. I want to tell you because I trust you and because you're close to me. [Pause] I am a lesbian—I am gay."

UNDERSTANDING YOUR FRIEND'S REACTION

From your knowledge of the gay community, gained through the research you did in Step 3 and through your friendships, you have learned a great deal about what it's like to be gay in America today. Your friend will probably have a lot of questions—perhaps the questions you envisioned—and you are able to answer them. Try to understand also that your news might be shocking to your friend, that your friend might be surprised or threatened.

"I could not believe that my friend Joe never suspected," notes Frank, a twenty-three-year-old writer who lives near Raleigh, North Carolina, and recently came out to his friends and family.

I thought he knew. I was sending out so many hints, hanging around with some friends who were pretty uninhibited—one was a drag queen by night who also wore makeup in the day and some pretty wild clothes. Joe used to see me with my gay friends a lot, in restaurants and stuff, but he never asked me about them. I thought that he probably figured it out but was respecting my privacy or something.

But then when I told him he was really surprised. I think he turned red. He got real bashful, sort of. He was trying not to be shocked but was shocked anyway, and he didn't know what to say. So I just let it kind of sink in for a while. I told him that we'd speak the next day.

I didn't hear from him for about four days. Then he called and asked me about a million questions. He was much better about the whole thing; he needed time, that's all.

Cynthia, a twenty-six-year-old Los Angeles medical student, remembers vividly her best friend's reaction:

Total, complete shock. She just said, "No! Really? No. Come on. Is this some kind of joke?" I was like, "It's no joke, honey," but I was laughing, because I kind of found the whole thing amusing in a way, so she still thought I was joking.

So then I just stayed quiet for a while. And I guess she was waiting for the punch line, for me to say that it was a put-on. But when I didn't, she finally said, "Wow, you're telling the truth, aren't you? Wow, okay, I can handle it," and then she went into the questions: "How long have you known?" "Why didn't you tell me before?" "Can we still be friends?" I couldn't believe she asked that question. It made me understand that a lot of straight people think it's the beginning of the end of a friendship, that you're abandoning them. I explained to her that this was really the beginning of a whole new friendship for us, where I wouldn't be lying and trying to cover up the real me.

It is a completely normal reaction for your friend to be surprised and need time to digest your news. As the testimonies of Cynthia's and Frank's friends demonstrate, this does not mean your friend can't or won't accept it. It just means that he or she may need some time. It's important for you to go back to your gay friends and talk about your straight friend's reactions so that you can get some responses and opinions that help you proceed.

IN CASE OF A BAD REACTION

If your friend reacts negatively or with hostility, or in a way different from how you envisioned, don't think of it as the end of the world. Many people react negatively at first and change over time, within days, weeks, or months. It is important to understand that a friend's negative reaction is a product of homophobia. Give your friend some space, and certainly don't match your friend's hostility and thus create a divisive and out-of-control situation. However, you must not accept any insults or other acts of homophobia that your friend foists upon you. Remember the Meditation Notes, particularly the second and the sixth:

- Homosexuality—as the American Psychiatric Association declared in 1973—is not a disease. Homophobia is a disease, like alcoholism or drug abuse.
- I can love those who are afflicted with homophobia and understand that they are not intentionally meaning to hurt me, but I must not let them harm me or affect my emotional well-being. I must reject all of their hatred toward homosexuals and understand that their hatred is their disease talking, even when those speaking are my teachers, my religious leaders, and my own family.

If your friend reacts negatively but exhibits respect for you, you might want to stay for a while and talk things through. But if your friend becomes abusive and insulting or if you simply reach a dead end in the discussion, it is important that you politely end the meeting. Tell your friend you're sorry he or she isn't accepting your news well and that it's best if you go now. Do not lose your cool or become nasty, no matter how ugly your friend becomes. It's important that your friend remember you as being calm and understanding. The last thing you want is for your friend to have a *real* reason to be angry with you, to use your flying off the handle or your meanness or rudeness as an excuse to be upset. This will only cloud the truth about your friend's homophobia.

Your friend either will change in time or will not. If your friend doesn't come around, you will have to understand that this person is so damaged by homophobia that he or she may be beyond help, at least for now. You will have to realize that this person is also selfish, and was perhaps not such a loyal friend in the first place: Those friends who really love you will try to overcome their fears or anxieties and accept you just as you are.

TURNING TO YOUR FAMILY OF FRIENDS

If your straight friends can't yet handle your news, turn to your new gay friends for support and guidance. You will be surprised how quickly your pain will pass. While you will feel sorrow at the loss of a friend, his or her reaction won't make you feel like less of a person.

As always, during this fragile time you should monitor your own reactions and watch out for the specter of self-loathing. It is important not to let a negative reaction keep you from going farther. You must prepare to come out to another straight friend as soon as possible. The only way to move on from a negative situation is to envision another, more positive one and, sadder but wiser, work again to make that situation happen.

And if your friend's reaction is positive and supportive, you probably feel a sense of liberation and relief. You probably feel that you are now ready, able, and eager to move ahead.

STEP 7

COMING OUT
TO OTHER FRIENDS

As you leave the closet farther behind and tell more and more of your friends, remember that everyone's reaction will be different. The responses you get may startle you, as they did Victor, a twenty-four-year-old dancer who lives in Las Vegas and who is still in the process of coming out to his friends. Victor says, "When I told my friend John back home in Iowa, he began crying and then hugged me, telling me that he too was gay."

Many people who are gay and closeted seem to become friends with other people who are gay and closeted. Perhaps unconsciously, they bond because of their mutual feelings of being alienated—even without knowing what commonalities have brought them together. When one comes out, the other often does too, either at the same time or later. Sometimes, even when a friend is not secretly gay, he or she might confide in you about some *other* secret long hidden from you. Your mutual relief and trust may draw the two of you even closer.

Because you have developed such respect for yourself,

you're now much better equipped to deal with any reactions you may get, including negative ones. Emboldened, you can now reach out to all those straight friends you thought might not embrace your news—except, of course, family members, which will happen later. You will have completed Step 7 when you have confided in all of your closest friends and processed all reactions you have received.

USING YOUR OWN JUDGMENT

You will have to use your own judgment in many cases. Some friends you may need to tell as a group, or perhaps separately but at the same time, because they are so close to each other and you.

George, a thirty-four-year-old New York artist, remembers that he felt compelled to tell a second straight friend almost immediately after he told the first. "Peter and Fred were my best friends when I was in college. We all grew up together in Queens, we all went to college locally, and we did *everything* together," he says.

I couldn't tell one of them and not tell the other. I told them separately. I told Peter first, while we went for a ride in his car. He was always more open-minded than Fred, and I thought it was better to tell him first so that if Fred couldn't handle it, Peter would be able to help him out. I told Peter—who was very cool about it—not to talk about it with Fred until I did, and that I planned to do it within the next few days. Then I told Fred, and he was cool about it too.

I then talked with both of them together and answered all the questions they had and told them not to tell anyone else or talk about it with anyone else until I did. That was cool with them, and they kind of liked watching me go about coming out to everyone—my family, their families, all of our other friends. They said that I had a lot of guts and they admired me for it.

After I talked with other people in our circles, then they did, so after a while everyone was talking with everyone else about it instead of having this big secret that everyone bottled up inside.

And that's a lot better way to live.

TIMING IS IMPORTANT

You may still want to tell all your friends at roughly the same time, even when they don't know one another, so that you can emotionally balance any negative responses with the ones that are positive and caring. Sheila, a twenty-three-year-old office temp who lives in a suburb of Chicago, remembers how different her second disclosure was compared to her first and third. But outing herself to a number of people within a two-week period took some of the sting out of the one negative reaction she received.

I was on a real high after telling my cousin Mel, who was the first straight person I came out to. He was very accepting and told me that he would do anything for me, *anything* that he could, that he wanted to help out in any way possible and that all I had to do was call him up and he'd be there.

But when I came out to my friend Judy a few days later, she was so cold and distant. She didn't want to talk about it, and that was that. I became depressed in a way because I had thought it would be just like with Mel. I called her up and tried to speak with her, but she was still distant.

That was over a year ago, and we've since become a bit friendlier—we got together a couple of times, went to a movie or two—but we're not really friends anymore. I mean, it's just not the same. She can't handle it, and I had to accept that.

I'm not going to let myself get bent out of shape about it. There's a chance she'll change, I guess, but to tell you the truth it's been so long now that I feel we've drifted apart and I don't really want her support now because she couldn't give it to me when I needed it the most.

It helped a lot that Mel had reacted great a few days earlier, because that made me feel good, and then I came out to Judy's sister about a week after I came out to Judy, and her being so supportive also helped a lot. It's funny because when I came out to Judy's sister Patty, who is just eighteen months younger than Judy and who is really kind of conservative—politically and personally—she was okay about it and even talked to me about Judy's problem dealing with it. She said, "I'm not sure how I feel about lesbians, and the gay-rights movement is something I can't say I fully support, but then again you're the first homosexual I've known and you're someone I like and I guess it's your right to be whoever you are and I should try to understand it."

Patty and I were always friendly, but never as close as Judy and I were. Now Patty and I are closer; we talk a lot on the phone and get together every so often, and we have a pretty good friendship. She genuinely respects me, even though she's still a bit uncomfortable and confused about the lesbian thing. But she's open to change.

EARNING A SECOND FAMILY OF FRIENDS

As Sheila's story illustrates, some people you think might respond positively will respond negatively, and vice versa.

As Sheila's story also shows, some people will simply move away from you emotionally while others, even some of those who have a problem with homosexuality and are victims of homophobia, will nonetheless become closer with you in a genuine attempt to understand you.

You will need all these experiences and more if you are going to comprehend all the complexities of homophobia. You must be prepared for any and all reactions that your parents and the rest of your family may have.

Coming out to a multitude of straight friends is vital, not only because you'll receive a lot of practice before you tell your family, but also because those who react positively will provide you with a second support group—a family of straight friends—you can rely on when you come out to relatives. You should come out to enough straight friends so that none of them feel that they are living in closets *about you*, unable to discuss openly the facts of your life. They will need to talk about this with others who are close to you. You should help your friends have friends they can talk to about your being gay.

Whenever you are contemplating coming out to a new person, go back to Step 6, reread the Envisioning passage, and perform Exercise 6, Envisioning. Use the Envisioning exercise to help create positive outcomes and to respond to any negative reactions.

KNOWING WHEN TO MOVE FORWARD

You'll know you have completed Step 7 when you feel that you have both a straight and a gay support group. Different people will need a different number of straight friends. What's important is that you feel that there are now no intimates—other than your family and your coworkers—who are unaware of your homosexuality. You'll need the support from straight friends so that you can see for yourself how comfortable straight people can be with your being gay.

Upon having completely mastered Part III of the Outing Yourself process, you should again take a break and assess your situation. You have come very far—much farther than many people who spend their lives trapped deeply in the closet. You probably are a happier and even healthier person for it. Once again, treat yourself to something beautiful, something enjoyable that will remind you of all the good associated with coming out.

You are now comfortable about being gay in both gay and straight social settings. You no longer feel that you have to hide. Though the prospect may seem difficult and anxiety-provoking, you'll know it's time to move forward when you need to complete the circle of honesty you are creating and include in your new life those people you care about most: your family.

PART IV

OUTING YOURSELF TO YOUR FAMILY

THAT FIRST TALK

Even if you were bursting to tell your straight friends that you are gay, you probably dread telling your family. This is natural. Friends may enjoy discovering new things about each other, but families have rigid and deep-seated expectations about the behavior and character of their members. Besides, we all want validation from our families, no matter how dysfunctional they are, and no one wants to disappoint them.

"Why is disclosing to the family such a problem for so many gay people?" asks therapist Betty Berzon.

We live in a family-oriented culture. Given the prolonged period of dependency on family in our society, the family becomes a highly influential force in our lives, from the cradle to the grave. We are trained to take on the values and attitudes of our families because it is more than the species the family is supposed to perpetuate, it is the value system of the culture supporting the nuclear family arrangement.

Even if your parents are liberal-minded and have even spoken supportively of gay people, it will still be difficult for them to accept that *you* are gay. Remember, they too have been raised in a homophobic society, coming of age in a time when homosexuality was even less understood and accepted than it is now.

While you might not be eager to tell your parents that you are gay, you have probably come to realize it is essential. This realization may be subtle: The self-loathing part of you will continue to whisper that it's not necessary to come out to your parents, but deep down you will know that hiding your true self is slowly eating away at you and making you feel shameful. You may even be in denial about how hiding your true self from your parents affects you.

"Often the psychic cost of concealing from your parents the information that you are same-sex-oriented is high," writes Mary V. Borhek in her book *Coming Out to Parents.*

> You are implicitly denying the worth of your true self and the worth of your relationship with your lover. You are living out the idea that a same-sex-oriented person *is* a second-class citizen and family member and that a relationship with a [same-sex] partner really *is* inferior to a relationship between married persons. This kind of self-disparagement is so subtle that you may not realize that it *is* disparaging.

If your parents love you and if they don't want the family to break apart, they will come to accept your homosexuality in time, no matter how they respond initially. It is impossible, however, to predict how families will react. Even liberal parents may react negatively, and often the most conservative parents will surprise you with their interest in your life and their support of your coming-out process.

"My parents have always been strict Jehovah's Witnesses," says Ronald, a thirty-one-year-old artist who lives in a rural area of Hawaii and is from a traditional Japanese-American family.

> When I first told them about myself, it was horrifying for them, especially reconciling it with their religion, the family, their friends. They didn't talk to me for a while, and then, perhaps when they realized that this is how I am and that I can't change, they seemed to suddenly accept it. Soon, my parents were meeting all of my gay friends, my mother was even cooking for them and being part of our social affairs. Both of them now have a true understanding of what gay is all about and they support me.

TELLING OTHER FAMILY MEMBERS

When we talk about discussing our homosexuality with our family, generally we mean outing ourselves to our parents first and then to other family members later. But this formula need not apply to everyone.

There are many reasons that parents may not be the first family members you need or want to talk to. Your parents may be far removed from your life, even living in a different city from you and other members of your immediate family; in some cases they may not still be living. You may, for example, be coming out later in life, after having been heterosexually married. If you are married with children and plan on divorcing your husband or wife, you probably feel that your immediate family should be told first.

"I did not come out until I was fifty-five, after both my parents had died within weeks of each other," says Mario, a sixty-five-year-old university professor who lives in a small town in Virginia.

For me, the big deal was coming out to my grown children and my wife. I had actually come out to her in the beginning of my marriage, only to be met with disbelief, incomprehension, and then hostility. Even today—after divorcing and coming out fully and leading an active gay life—she professes not to believe that I am "really" gay.

Coming out to my children, on the other hand, was not difficult. What was difficult on all of us was the separation and the divorce—and my leaving home. I told them individually—four daughters and one son—and they all rather quickly accepted it. They are marvelous, sophisticated people.

If this situation or a similar one applies to you, you can find support groups and books dealing with how to come out to children, husbands, and wives. Check with local gay community centers, gay and lesbian groups, and libraries and bookstores. Two books that have useful chapters on coming out to your children are *Reinventing the Family: The Emerging Story of Lesbian and Gay Parents*, by Laura Benkov, Ph.D. (New York: Crown, 1994), and *The Lesbian and Gay Parenting Handbook: Creating and Raising Our Families*, by April Martin, Ph.D. (New York: HarperCollins, 1993). While all of the steps in *Outing Yourself* will be helpful to you, you should also seek support for your individual circumstance. Since for most people the first family members they out themselves to will be parents, Step 8 will focus on this major component of outing yourself.

There are, however, other reasons why your parents may not be the first family members to whom you out yourself. You may be very close with siblings and feel you can confide in them. You might have already spoken to one or more brothers or sisters. If you haven't, you still might feel more comfortable talking with them before talking with the rest of your family.

In Step 6 it was suggested that if a sibling is truly your best friend, you might want to come out to him or her early on; in these cases, siblings should be treated more like friends than like parents, and you should follow the procedures discussed in Steps 6 and 7 about coming out to friends. You will have to make this decision based on your particular relationship with your brothers and/or sisters. Every family is different. Remember, however, that your siblings may feel the need to tell your parents. Unlike your friends, no matter how much your siblings love and understand you, and no matter how much they want you to confide in them, they will react to your coming out in a more personal way than your friends will: They will feel that your being gay reflects on them.

"My brother immediately became anxious because he thought that he might be gay too, saying that we have the same genes and that even if homosexuality was caused environmentally, we still were brought up in the same environment and therefore he might be gay," recalls Sara, a twenty-one-year-old Portland, Oregon, student.

> This was paranoid and silly, I thought. I know that if it was one of his friends, he'd not have reacted weirdly at all. He's generally really accepting and he was trying to be in this case, but his fears were getting the best of him. He wanted to tell my parents, because he said he needed to talk it over with them, and he was pushing me to talk with them. I realized I had to, for his sake, even though I wasn't ready at that point. I was afraid he'd go and out me himself. Even though it pretty much worked out, it was a mistake to tell him first, because it caused me all this grief and anxiety that was

totally unnecessary and forced me to go to my parents
before I really wanted to.

In general, you will find that it is probably wiser to tell
your parents first, and then go on to siblings and others in
the family. In this way, too, your parents will not feel con-
spired against, as if they are always "the last to know"—a
common complaint among parents in regard to a child's
coming out as well as other issues.

UNDERSTANDING YOUR PARENTS

As with previous steps for outing yourself, you will have
to do some preliminary work for Step 8. The approach
you take with your parents will have to be different from
the one you took when you outed yourself to friends.
Some things, like the Envisioning exercise, will be the
same, but *how* you envision outing yourself—and how you
eventually do it—will be different.

Most parents have expectations of their children, straight
or gay, that children can rarely meet. Even those parents
who give their children a great deal of independence often
see their children as an extension of themselves, as a *part of
them*—a part that they sometimes view as reliving their
own lives. ("I felt that too when I was your age, but it went
away.") It is often hard on parents when their children
don't meet their expectations; parents may simply feel as if
a *part of them* has not lived up to their standards.

Therefore, unlike when your straight friends found out
about your sexuality, your parents will feel as if they are
being told that a *part of them* is homosexual. Your friends,
whether they reacted positively or negatively, reacted to
you as an entity outside of themselves and probably didn't
personalize your disclosure—unless, of course, your
friends are also gay and closeted.

But your parents may feel upon your coming out very

much the way *you* may have felt when you first realized you might be gay. They may be stunned and even grief-stricken and may react with intense sadness, anger, revulsion, or fear. Remember, just as you felt when you realized you were gay, they will be confronted with the loss of the old you. They will have to get over the initial shock and *mourn* that person before they can accept the new you. And since they view you as a *part of them*, this loss will be almost as profound for them as if a part of themselves were dying.

For this reason, they will not receive your news with ease—no matter how much you preface it by saying your revelation is something that you believe is wonderful and worth rejoicing over. They simply won't feel happy for you—at first; they will be much too preoccupied with their own grief. Unlike your friends, who are more objective and can understand and accept your celebratory approach to coming out, you will need to envision and ultimately perform your coming out to your parents in a much more neutral and goal-oriented way.

WHEN, WHERE, HOW

Parents should generally be told together, even perhaps if they no longer are married to each other. It's important that you not appear to be playing favorites by confiding in one and not the other. It's also important that you not allow either of them to use you or this issue as a way of exercising control by withholding information from others in the family, a common occurrence. If it is impossible to out yourself to both parents together—perhaps because they are divorced and do not speak, or because they live in different cities—you should tell one fairly soon after you've told the other, within days if possible. Make sure to let the first parent you inform know that you are telling the other the same information. Do not let that parent talk you out of telling the other—no matter what, even if he or she says, as so many parents do, "It will kill your father/mother." There are no confirmed cases of heart failure induced by disclosure of a child's homosexuality.

You should come out to your parents in a place where you can all be comfortable and have complete privacy. A restaurant is usually *not* appropriate; it will make your parents uncomfortable to be confronted with this news in public, and it may indicate to them that you are not concerned about *their* reaction because you did not afford them privacy for a disclosure they find embarrassing. If you and your parents don't live together, choose either their place or your place, wherever you think they will be most comfortable and wherever you will have the most privacy.

Remember: While with the first straight friend you told you may have gone out to dinner at a favorite restaurant to celebrate your disclosure, you should not give your parents the impression that you are celebrating anything. It's not appropriate to invite them for a dinner in which you cook their favorite meal—this too may signal some sort of celebration, and the gesture will undoubtedly be lost on them anyway after the disclosure. Be point-blank and emotionally neutral about the meeting's importance and formality: "I'd like us to meet so that I can talk about something that's important to me. We'll need some time and some privacy."

If your parents try to pump you for advance information, especially by asking, "Why? Is there anything wrong?" you should resist giving your news away—or giving them any hints whatsoever—while at the same time trying not to scare them or to diminish the importance of the conversation. It's best to respond with something like the following: "It's not a question of right or wrong, but we really shouldn't discuss it right now. It's important and we'll need some time, which is why I would like to wait until we meet before I tell you anything else about it."

If they pump you further or try to guess, continue to refuse politely to tell them anything further until the meeting—even if by chance they guess correctly.

It's best to talk about your homosexuality with parents (and others) at a time when there are no family crises or traumas, such as the sickness or death of a loved one. It's also wise not to tell them during busy, festive times, such as just before or on Thanksgiving, Christmas, or other holidays that your family celebrates together. Not only are people preoccupied with many things just before and on the holidays, but it is a time when families come together to connect and often when nerves are raw for all. Introducing potential conflict on these days of bonding and celebration will probably only anger your parents; they will see it as disrespectful of them, as discourteous, and as "throwing it in their faces." The days directly following the holiday, however, when many families are still together but the anxiety of the "big day" is gone, are good, comparatively stress-free times to have this first talk.

As you did with your friends, make sure you have enough time to deal with the ensuing questions your parents will have. You might also want to have some books on hand specifically for and about parents of lesbians and gay men that your parents can read, or have a list of books they might want to pick up themselves. These might include *Now That You Know: What Every Parent Should Know About Homosexuality* (revised edition), by Betty Fairchild and Nancy Hayward (Orlando, Fla.: Harcourt Brace Jovanovich, 1989), *Beyond Acceptance: Parents of Lesbians and Gays Talk About Their Experience*, by Carolyn Welch Griffin, Marian J. Wirth, and Arthur G. Wirth (New York: St. Martin's Press, 1990), and *The Family Heart: A Memoir of When Our Son Came Out*, by Robb Forman Dew (Reading, Mass.: Addison-Wesley, 1994). You might also want to have the telephone number of your local chapter of Parents, Family, and Friends of Lesbians and Gays (their national office in Washington can give you a local number; call [202] 638-4200) just in case your parents are ready and able to seek outside support from others who've gone through the same experience.

Before talking with your parents, you should complete Exercise 7, Re-envisioning, as often as you need to.

EXERCISE 7: RE-ENVISIONING

We call this exercise Re-envisioning because we are going to change the Envisioning exercise from Exercise 6 slightly to apply to your parents. Go back to Step 6 and read the Envisioning passage (page 66). The only difference between Envisioning Exercise 6 and Exercise 7 is that now you will not envision coming out in a celebratory manner, but rather more neutrally.

Sit down in a comfortable spot and ponder coming out to your parents.

Picture the place: a familiar setting that you all are comfortable in. Their house or apartment, or perhaps yours. Or maybe a fairly empty public park or nearby wooded area. A quiet place where you can have some privacy.

Envision yourself in a upbeat mood, not nervous, anxious, or sad. You are confiding in your parents because you want to share something about yourself that you feel they should know because they are close to you. You are not telling them in order for them to celebrate with you, but rather so that you will not live in hiding any longer.

Picture yourself saying: "Mom and Dad, there's something important I want to tell you. I'm telling you because you're among the closest people in my life, and I think it would be wrong for me to hide a part of myself from you any longer. I'm a lesbian. (I'm gay.)"

Think about how your parents might respond positively to what you say. What would a positive response be? What would they do? What questions would they have?

Create the scenario that describes the most positive outcome you can imagine. Write it down. Fill in as much detail as possible. Where exactly are you meeting? What are you wearing? What time is it? How much time will you spend together? What will you do afterward?

Go over the scenario again and again until it becomes second nature.

Let its positive feelings fill you deeply.

For the next few days, or however long it takes, go to a quiet place a few times each day, and envision the scenario again. During these days or weeks, whenever negative thoughts about coming out enter into your mind, whenever your mind begins to construct a negative scenario, whenever you see mental images of your parents reacting negatively or with hostility, stop yourself and envision the positive. Put the negative thoughts out of your mind by envisioning your positive scenario. This effort requires diligence and perseverance.

You are, of course, trying to create a new and positive self-fulfilling prophecy. Think about all the aspects of your created scenario that make it a positive one. Think about what you can do to make it happen.

Think about what conditions in your envisioned scenario—the setting, the day, the time, your parents' mood, your own mood—will need to be duplicated in real life in order to have that positive outcome.

Think about how you will do that.

MAINTAINING YOUR TONE

Your frame of mind and your behavior are of ultimate importance when you are outing yourself to parents.

Remember, you are telling them something that they are not prepared for, although you yourself have had a lot of time to prepare. Their volatile reactions to this shocking news are understandable when you consider how homophobic our culture is. However they react, you won't ultimately benefit if you respond to their grief or anger in an equally negative or angry way.

David, a thirty-two-year-old Chicago-based flight attendant, remembers how his behavior affected his coming-out process when he came out to his parents at the age of twenty-eight:

At first everything seemed okay. I hadn't visited with them in a while and they were happy to see me. We sat down in the living room, and I said I had something important to tell them about myself. They were very eager to hear about it; they always liked hearing news about my life, and so I said something like, "Well, Mom and Dad, I love you both, and so I think you should know, so that you can be closer to me and understand me, that I am gay. I have a partner, and we'll be moving in together, and I'd like you to meet him."

Now, my parents are both first-generation Chinese-Americans; even though they both grew up in this country, they still live very traditionally and have lived their lives, more or less, according to how their parents wanted them to. They have of course taken on some American customs and practices that their parents were not happy about, but generally they've lived in a conservative, traditional way compared to most other people and certainly compared to me and my generation. What I had just said was completely at odds with what they wanted of me for my life.

My father said nothing and got up and left the room, and my mother started crying. I became angry and started yelling, telling them they've never loved me and that they've always wanted to mold me into their idea of the perfect son. I called them dinosaurs and said they needed to get out of the Stone Age.

I said a lot of things just to make them feel bad.

I was of course demanding that they get over centuries of tradition inside of a minute—not to mention the fact that this so-called "modern Western culture" is also homophobic. By getting angry and upset with them I was making a painful revelation more painful for them. It was a few weeks before we could even broach the subject again.

Looking back, I know that if I hadn't blown up and said a lot of hurtful things my father would probably have eventually come back into the room after the initial shock was over, and my mom would have stopped crying and would have wanted to discuss it further. But it seemed I was determined to hurt them.

It was part of that sort of rage that you first feel when you wake up and see how everybody's antigay attitudes have really hurt you for so long.

"I was just, like, ready to burst out and explode when I told my parents," says Libby, a seventeen-year-old Detroit high school student who recently came out to her mother and father.

I didn't have the time to go into it and I didn't care to. My attitude was like, "You should *already* be totally non-homophobic. Why should I have to educate you?" I was just really mad at them for being part of this homophobic planet and for saying that they love me while at the same time making fun of gay people and not knowing that I was one. I was, like, ready to totally boil over. Then I finally did.

One night, I walked in and I was late and they were,

like, "Where have you been?" And I was, like, "With my *girlfriend*, as in like, I have sex with her, okay? I'm a lesbian, Mom. A *lesbian*. L-E-S-B-I-A-N. Get it? And I'm sick of taking bullshit."

They were just, like, floored. There was screaming and fighting and throwing things. And I had to stay at my aunt's house for a few days. I was just so defiant and I did it in a mean way. It all was really dumb and imma- ture. I wasn't caring about them. It was all about me, me, me.

The temptation may be great, but try not to do it like Libby.

CHECKING YOUR ANGER

It's understandable if you are pent up with anger and feel impatient. You've spent your whole life denying your true self, hiding from those whom you love. Your parents, themselves victims of homophobia, were part of that— and they certainly did not encourage you to be your true self or offer you the option of living openly gay *in case* you were homosexual. It is natural for you to see them as par- tially having caused you to live in the closet.

By coming out to yourself and learning about the gay community, you have probably come to realize that you were in effect lied to about homosexuality. Now that you have gay friends—perhaps you are even involved with someone in a relationship—and now that you have come out to straight friends as well, you probably have a confi- dence that is buttressed only by anger. You probably feel that you will allow *no one* to make you feel bad about yourself—and that includes your parents.

This defiant attitude is natural and healthy. It means that you have been progressing well, challenging those who would have you hate yourself. But if you are now going to come out to your parents in a productive way, you must check that anger and resentment, summon up all of the patience you have, and understand that your parents' attitudes are a product of their homophobia. Do not, however, *tell* them that they are victims of homophobia or inform them that they are suffering from a disease. Any accusations, charges, or labels will only make them defensive. Your goal should be to inform them about yourself and to break the news to them gently, without targeting them or accusing them of any bad behavior, no matter how angry you are at them or how angry they may become with you.

MAINTAINING A POSITIVE APPROACH

Just as in telling your straight friends, when you come out to your parents you should not appear sad or upset. You don't want to appear inappropriately celebratory, but you don't want to give the impression that you are uncomfortable with being gay or that you have not thought out the implications of your new life or reasons for telling them about it. Any display of negative emotions will set the tone for how your parents react. You may be seeking sympathy from them because of the homophobia you have suffered—and thus you may feel like crying. If you do, they may indeed sympathize with you—but for a different reason: They may feel that it is your *homosexuality* that is upsetting you, especially since that is what will upset *them*.

When you perform Exercise 7, Re-envisioning, think about how you will tell your parents about your homosexuality. Think about your tone of voice and your attitude. When you have finished the Re-envisioning exercise, repeat the following vows to yourself:

VOWS FOR COMING OUT TO PARENTS

- I vow not to appear sad, lonely, or dejected when I out myself to my parents.
- I vow to sympathize with my parents' pain, and help them in any way I can to understand my homosexuality, including answering all of their questions.
- I vow to understand that my parents may need some time alone and that I at some point should perhaps defer further discussion until a later date.
- I vow to comprehend that my parents will not accept me right away or support me, but I will believe that our relationship and their understanding of my homosexuality can and will grow in time.

EXERCISE 8: TWENTY QUESTIONS

After you have done the Re-envisioning exercise and pictured the place, the mood, and your parents' reaction, and after you have recited the Vows for Coming Out to Parents, sit down in a quiet place with a pen and paper.

Think about the questions that they may ask about your being gay, even if they seem to you to be ridiculous questions.

Remember: Your parents are very much in the dark about homosexuality.

Write down the questions, leaving some space for answers. Your paper should look something like this:

How do you know you're gay?

How long have you known?

Do you have AIDS?

Do you blame us?

Can you be "cured"?

After you have come up with twenty questions that your parents might ask, write down the answers to the questions, fleshing out your thoughts thoroughly. To get accurate answers, you might have to go back to the library, or back to some of the books you have read. You might try to include references to famous gay people past and present, so that your parents will have some immediate context for understanding how homosexuals have thrived in the world.

Try to include references that are familiar to them so that your being gay does not seem foreign or bizarre. Maybe you can talk about the great American writer Walt Whitman or the champion tennis player Martina Navratilova. You might want to talk about people in your own community whom your parents respect and who are out of the closet unbeknownst to your parents.

DON'T BE HARD ON YOURSELF

When you do the Re-envisioning exercise, as well as when you finally sit down and talk to your parents, you will have to give yourself some leeway, depending on the personalities and attitudes of both yourself and your parents. Obviously you should not follow these suggestions so rigidly that your coming out seems stilted or rehearsed; not every piece of advice will apply to your situation. You will have to go with what feels right, knowing that things won't go exactly as you planned. Whatever happens, don't be depressed or angry with yourself if you change your plan as you go along to suit yourself and your parents, or if your actual coming out does not go exactly according to plan. Each individual's coming-out process is different.

"I decided I would tell my family when I was home on

fall break," remembers Gregory, a twenty-year-old South
Dakota student.

Unfortunately, I didn't. Each night I would go to bed
and get myself all psyched up to tell them, but each day
I would lose my courage at the sight of them. I was
courageous in theory but not in practice. One evening,
I even went into my parents' room and told them I had
something very important I wanted to talk about. After
that evening, in addition to not knowing their son was
gay, they now thought—totally erroneously—I was
close to flunking out of school. Needless to say, I went
back to school without telling them and I felt really bad
about that.

The good thing was that Thanksgiving was not too
far off and we were all meeting at my uncle's house in
Minneapolis. My father's gay brother and his partner
were going to be there, so I figured that would give me
strength. On Friday night [after Thanksgiving], our last
night in Minneapolis, I sat in the room my parents were
staying in as they packed up their things. We made idle
conversation, talking about the weekend and such, but
nothing too terribly important.

I had decided the night before that I was not going
to leave for school without them knowing I was gay. I
had considered telling them earlier in the day, when the
three of us were at a restaurant having lunch, but it was
not very private so I decided against that. I waited until
they had finished packing and had both gotten into bed.

Then, somehow knowing that I had something I
wanted to talk about, my mother asked, "Is there something you want to talk about?" I said yes, and after
thinking about it for a few seconds, I said, "Mom and
Dad, I'm gay," and proceeded to break into tears
against my will.

I had told myself over and over that I had to be

strong when I came out to them, showing them that this was a good thing. But even the best ideas are not always realistic.

We talked for about two hours that night, covering many issues. The two that I remember most clearly are HIV/AIDS (my mother asked me to promise her I would never die of AIDS—I told her I couldn't promise her that, but I would try my hardest not to and that she should have the same worry about my straight brother) and my father's inability to understand how I could know I am gay if I had never been sexually active with another man. The night ended with them telling me they loved me and that it would take some time for them to get accustomed to the fact that their son is gay.

Through the next year, as a family we struggled to meet each other on our own terms. I wanted them to be totally okay with the idea right away, and they were worried that I was too out publicly. In the end, it was just that we were at different points in the coming-out process, and it was unfair for any of us to expect each other to accelerate or retard that process to accommodate ourselves.

One evening that January, when I was home for winter break, my parents called me into their room after a discussion—well, a fight—we had about the issue of my sexuality. My mother said, "We just want you to know that the reason we are struggling with this is that we are afraid of losing you. We don't want this issue to cause us to drift apart. And if there is anyone who has a problem with your being gay, they are no longer our friends. And that includes members of our extended family."

Gregory's story illustrates how things don't necessarily have to go 100 percent according to plan for results eventually to be satisfactory. But the fact that he made a plan, and followed it to the best of his ability, definitely aided in his coming out to his parents in the best possible way, a way that would lead to the most positive results.

When Gregory decided to tell his parents during his fall break, he had already come up with his plan. While his inability to initiate the discussion made him feel that he was not "courageous," it really only meant that he wasn't ready and that he was being cautious and methodical about his coming out. This is wise. He was envisioning his coming out to his parents and he wasn't ready to do so.

He'd also decided, wisely, to have that first talk on the day *after* Thanksgiving, after the actual stress and business of the holiday had ended. He also wisely decided against coming out to them over lunch, in a restaurant.

Gregory was also able to answer his parents' questions. While parts of the process did not go as he had envisioned—he hadn't meant to cry, for instance—Gregory had planned his coming out, and *enough* of it went according to plan that any missteps did not affect the outcome adversely. We cannot control other people's reactions, and we can control our own only to a degree.

ANXIETY

After you have prepared for some time, after you have envisioned your coming out to your parents and after you can thoroughly answer the twenty questions, you will know you are ready to speak to your parents. You might now want to give yourself a deadline or a challenge. Gregory, for example, told himself he was not going to go back to school after his Thanksgiving break without having told his parents that he is gay.

It is normal for you at this time to be affected by anxiety, especially when you are in your parents' presence, thinking about how you want to tell them you are gay. Everyone who has come out has felt the same feelings.

"I used to get that horrible nervous stomach, that queasy feeling, and that tingling all over my body just at the thought of talking about this to my mother and father," says Andrea, a twenty-eight-year-old retail clerk who lives in Gainesville, Florida. "It's that terrible feeling that runs through your body when you know that something you've dreaded is upon you. I've had friends who've gotten physically ill about telling their parents that they are gay."

It's important to know you are not alone in feeling such anxiety and that you cannot let it stop you from proceeding with your task. Take a few deep breaths and put negative thoughts out of your mind. If the anxiety is so overwhelming that it impairs your effort to come out, you might want to see a counselor or therapist.

THE BIG DAY

When the day (or evening) has arrived in which you will have that first talk, be sure that you are not in a bad mood, and try to make sure that you are rested. If, for whatever reason, you have had a bad day or lost a lot of sleep— perhaps because you were nervous about the big day—try to postpone your announcement rather than plunge into it while you are not physically and emotionally equipped to deal with the reactions you will get.

Before the meeting, make sure to dress and look the way you usually do: Wearing provocative clothes or T-shirts with gay slogans on them will only threaten your parents further. You do not want them to think you have been transformed from their daughter or son into whatever it is they believe homosexuals are. You don't want to further whatever suspicions they have that gay people are "recruited." You want them to know that they are looking at the same son or daughter they've always known, except of course that a new dimension of you—which you are telling them has always been there—is being revealed for the first time.

When you are finally ready to say what you need to say, proceed as you did in Exercise 7, Re-envisioning. Again, for everyone it will be different, but a standard approach is to say: "Mom and Dad, there's something important I want to tell you. I'm telling you because you're among the closest people in my life, and I think it would be wrong for me to hide a part of myself from you any longer. I'm a lesbian—I am gay."

DEALING WITH PARENTAL REACTIONS

It's unlikely but possible that your parents might actually accept your being gay right away. In these cases, either they suspected that you were gay a long time ago and faced that reality and overcame their fears, or you are unusually lucky and they were never victims of homophobia and view gays and lesbians without bias.

It is more likely, however, that your parents will not react positively at first—at least not as positively as you would like. Their initial reactions may include any and all of the following: Shock: "I'm speechless." Confusion: "I don't understand what you're saying." Denial: "No, it's not true, you are *not* gay." Guilt: "This is all my fault." Finger-pointing: "This is because we sent you away to school." Sadness: "I feel as if my child is dead." Revulsion: "It's disgusting." Anger: "How *could you* do this to us!" Some parents may express any of the above, or other reactions, while at the same time assuring you that they love you and that they'll try deal with your homosexuality and understand it. Others may say that they will never accept it or that they refuse to discuss it further.

Whatever your parents' reaction, don't take it to heart

just yet. These are just initial reactions to what for them is shocking and unpleasant news. Your parents need time to digest what you have said. Their attitudes, whether positive or negative, can—and often do—swing 180 degrees over time. Often they will swing back and forth several times. It will be quite a while before your parents reach closure on this issue, no matter what they say now.

If your parents seem genuinely interested in finding out more, now is the time to answer their questions in the ways you had practiced during the Twenty Questions exercise, and even offer them books on the subject and telephone numbers of groups such as P-Flag so they can call for information and support. However, if they appear stunned, distraught, disengaged, angry, or sad, it may be best to respond *briefly* to their pressing concerns, and then to let the meeting end so that all of you will have time to think about what was said. Those pressing concerns may range from their thinking that they "caused" you to be gay, to fears (and perhaps misconceptions) about AIDS, to asking if you were molested as a child, to deciding that if all gay men and lesbians are child molesters, therefore you must be one too. Remember to be understanding and patient. If they talk about your gayness being their "fault," explain to them, as you learned in your research, that homosexuality is no one's "fault" and that it is a myth that parents can "cause" children to be gay. If they begin to speak of trying to seek a "cure," explain, as you have learned, that homosexuality is not a disease and therefore can't be cured. Explain to them that, in spite of what they may have heard, gay people cannot be changed into heterosexuals—*just as straight people cannot be changed into homosexuals.*

If they are crying, let them cry.

If they are angry, let them be angry.

Your pleas to them to stop crying or to stop being angry

will insult them, because you would be downplaying the magnitude of what you have said. You might say instead: "This is difficult, I know. It wasn't easy for me when I first realized I was gay. I think we all need a bit of space. Let's talk again at another time." Right now, they need someone to sympathize with their pain, and although it might be the last thing you feel you want to do, it is important that you connect with them. You are all they have at this moment, and they probably feel as if they've lost you.

End your first talk by keeping communication open, no matter how badly or how well it may have gone. Even if your parents reacted well, they may still be harboring fears that they did not express. Sometimes there is a delayed reaction. It is important in these cases that you acknowledge to your parents that they may have different feelings and a lot of questions later on, and that you'd like to talk again. As you will see in Step 9, this first talk is only the very beginning of a larger discussion that will take place over a much longer time.

AFTER YOUR PARENTS

After you out yourself to your parents, you should move on to others in the family to whom you are still closeted, such as siblings, cousins, aunts, uncles, and grandparents, depending on how close you are to them. You should do this at your own pace, but don't take too long. If your parents are still uneasy they may try to keep you from telling others, and the longer you don't tell others the longer your parents will view this as a "dirty little secret" that you are helping them to keep.

You may find that simply by having told your parents, the entire process becomes remarkably easy when you out yourselves to others.

"I found it so much easier to tell my brothers after I

told my parents," remembers Todd, a thirty-five-year-old San Francisco banking executive who grew up in Utah, in a conservative Mormon family.

> It's like the cat is finally out of the bag, and you realize that the reason you were really so worried about telling everyone else is that you were afraid that your parents would eventually find out. After your parents know, there's such a burden lifted.
>
> I was concerned that my brothers—three of them, all older than me—would not accept me. But that wasn't really true. The oldest one accepted it right away and said he'd always known. The other two seemed a bit distant, but I think they love me no matter what and will get used to it. It's only been a year now and they're rather conservative and take time to digest things. I know that one of the reasons they respect me so much and accept my being gay is that I had the integrity and courage to sit down and tell my parents about it.

Generally, follow the same guidelines in coming out to other relatives that you followed for parents: envisioning and checking your anger. Everyone will react differently and you should be prepared for the variety of responses.

"I thought my sister Nancy would take it real well—I even had thought she might be a lesbian herself," recalls Victoria, a twenty-seven-year-old Tampa lifeguard.

> But she took it bad, much worse than my parents, and she even tried to convince them that they should not allow me back in the house until I "went straight." She's come a long way since then, but that initial reaction really shocked me. I guess my impulsive reaction would have been to get real angry with her and start a big fight. But instead, I allowed her to carry on and cry

and complain to others about it, and I tried to just be supportive and talk to others in the family about her reaction. It was a time of great concern in the family. People were concerned for me, and they were concerned for her too, and they all tried to make things better. One of my cousins even forced my sister and me to sit down in her kitchen and talk. That was the beginning of our really discussing this, and I realized that Nancy needed to vent for a while and get over her shock. It worked out in the long run, but you have to be prepared for just about anything in the beginning.

As Victoria's story shows, initial reactions may often surprise you. But remember: They are not necessarily an indication of how a relative will ultimately handle your homosexuality; they may simply be impulsive responses to shocking news. Understand that many people will need time to get over their shock. This step is simply about getting the truth out in the open.

While some family members may surprise you with their negative reactions, others may surprise you with positive ones.

"I would never in a million years think that my grandmother would accept this," notes Salvatore, a thirty-seven-year-old Baltimore store owner.

We come from an Italian Catholic family, and she's very religious. She's also eighty-one years old, and the world was a lot different when she was young. I don't think homosexuality was even something people whispered about. I was not planning on telling her that I was gay, because I thought it would destroy her—my mother actually said that, and convinced me not to tell my grandmother. But then one day I was visiting her while she was watching her soap operas, and she said to me, "Isn't that man beautiful?," pointing to an actor on the TV. I looked at her kind of funny and she said, "I'm not stupid, you know, I know you don't like girls." And then she smiled, and she said, "I watch all of the talk shows, I know what's going on in the world." I said to her, "Grandma, I'm gay, and I was afraid to tell you." She said, "Sal, when you get to be my age a lot of things don't bother you that used to bother you. You realize that a lot of things aren't important enough to get upset over. What's important is that people are happy."

LOOKING BACK AT YOUR ACCOMPLISHMENTS

After you come out to your parents and other family members, dealing with their initial reactions and tabling further discussion for the moment, you will have completed the most anxiety-provoking step in the Outing Yourself process. Congratulations.

It's important now to sit back and assess what you have done. Go back and talk to your gay family and friends as well as your straight friends about what happened. Look to them for encouragement, support, and advice.

No matter how your parents may have responded, celebrate with your friends the fact that you are no longer lying to the two people who have been the most influential in your life. You will now do the best you can to mend any strain that your disclosure has put on your relationship with your parents and other family members. No matter how hurt they may be, you did what was ultimately the right and most responsible thing to do—for yourself as well as for your family.

KEEPING THE DISCUSSION GOING

"It seemed as if everything went fine at first—no real uproar and lots of support," recalls Ann, a thirty-six-year-old Washington, D.C., computer technician, regarding her coming out to her family.

> Everyone in my family—my mother, my father, my sister, my brother—they've always been liberals and very proud of it. They'd never *say* anything homophobic. But I guess I fooled myself into believing that meant they didn't harbor any homophobia. And that's ridiculous to believe when you think about it, because *everyone's* homophobic. It's the way we're taught. I even said to my parents, "Look, if you have a problem with this, it's okay to talk about it." And they said, "Oh, no, we don't have a problem. Not at all."
>
> But soon after I told my parents, it was like they didn't want to know anything more. Soon, they were never asking me questions about my life and the people in it and didn't seem to want to hear about it when

I'd bring things up. The same thing happened not too long after I came out to my sister and her husband, and it even happened with my little brother, who seemed the most accepting.

It was as if I had told them something that was so shameful that after confessing it, you don't talk about it because it just wouldn't be proper. I felt as if I'd gone back into the closet.

Michael, a twenty-six-year-old photographer who lives in an Oklahoma town, recalls how his parents reacted with great anger and fear when he came out to them two years ago; then they became what he perceived as supportive, only to eventually try to ignore his homosexuality completely:

My father spit at me and said he never wanted to see me again. My mother cried and said I was now "in the hands of Satan." They're evangelical Christians, and this was the worst thing imaginable as far as they were concerned.

I had told them point-blank that I was gay and that I couldn't and wouldn't change. I did not get angry back at them—I just left the house, went to my apartment, and invited some friends over to talk about it. It had me down, but I had my friends and they really helped me through it.

Over the next few weeks, my mother called several times, asking a lot of questions about gay issues. Finally, she said that my father wanted to talk with me also, so I went to their house and we had a long discussion, and they seemed to eventually accept my homosexuality. They still hadn't accepted it in a religious sense—I think they still thought it was a terrible affront to God—but they realized that the choice was now between trying to change their attitude over time and get used to the idea or lose their son, and I think they loved me too much to let me go. They said that as long as I was happy, they could accept me and that they'd try to understand my new life. But they really didn't mean that because that was it, as far as talking about my being gay.

They never talked to me about it again, and every time I tried to talk about it, they changed the subject. I really don't feel welcome in their home, even though they want me there all the time. That's because the person they really want there is the old me—the closeted me. This new me, the out and proud me, is not someone they really want to get to know.

Ann's and Michael's experiences are common. Whether or not parents and other family members take the news well at first, they need to be reminded about your being gay or else they will sink into denial. Don't forget: They were in a closet of sorts too, as the parents, brother, sister, or other relative of a gay man or lesbian. You have lived within the gay community for a reasonable amount of time now, but all they possess are a lot of myths and misconceptions. You've now brought out in the open something with which they have little or no practical experience. They don't even possess the vocabulary to talk about gay issues.

They're probably not used to talking about sexuality in general, and they will see your being gay as a very *sexual* topic, even if you never discuss sex at all. You probably see it as being about your identity, about who you are, but your parents, your brothers, sisters, aunts, uncles, and cousins will assume that all you want to discuss with them is sex. There is much that they will have to learn, and that will come from their continued interaction with you. They must eventually come to an understanding that this is not some dark, dirty secret—this is your life. The only way they learn this is by talking about your life, and the only way they will continue talking about your life is if *you* keep the discussion going.

SETTING THE RULES OF DISCUSSION

Again, check your anger when you see that your family is going back into the closet about your being gay. You probably feel that, now that you have come out, your parents should incorporate your gayness into the family and have as deep an interest in it as they have in the lives of your heterosexual siblings or cousins. But just because they are not talking about it doesn't mean they are not interested; more likely it means that they don't know what is proper to say, how to broach certain topics without feeling as if they are prying, or what you expect from them.

It is imperative that you go out of your way to define the rules of discourse about your homosexuality—which should be similar to the rules of discourse for heterosexuality.

Discuss your homosexuality *as often as they discuss their heterosexuality:* Talk about your circle of friends, about how some are settling down in couples, some are going to a gay-singles ski weekend, some are being promoted at work, some are contemplating having children. Describe your new boyfriend or girlfriend. Tell them about the gay volleyball league you've joined or the lesbian bowling team. It's important for them to know that, just like straight people, you and other gay people of similar likes and dislikes get together in a variety of ways. It's important they understand that, contrary to the myths they might believe, your life is no more about sex than are the lives of most heterosexuals.

"My parents really were at square one in all of this," says Marilyn, a thirty-three-year-old insurance salesperson who lives in a rural area of southern Indiana.

They were furious with me for weeks after I told them, but I know I made it worse by being so angry with them for not understanding immediately. After things died down a bit, my brother called me and wanted to know if I was coming home for Thanksgiving. He had been trying to get me to reconcile with them and said my parents really wanted me there. So I called my mother and said I was coming. On the telephone she seemed so happy and excited that I was coming, but we didn't talk about my being a lesbian or about anything like that. Throughout the entire weekend it never came up, even when I was alone with my father and mother.

I left and went home and felt like it was all so hopeless. They would never accept me, I kept thinking to myself. And I knew that I couldn't keep going there and living in silence—especially since I'd already come out to them. I was just miserable and spent a lot of time crying.

So I called up my mother and I said, "Mom, we didn't discuss once during the entire weekend the news I told you several weeks ago about my being a lesbian. It caused a big breakup with us and had us not talking, and when I finally came home we didn't talk about it at all."

She replied, "What is there to talk about? You told us. You said it's not *your* fault. You said it's not *our* fault. You said it's not something you can change, and that you're much happier this way than trying to live in a way you feel is not right for you. After reading up on the subject, those are all things we now probably agree with. So what is there to talk about? We're trying to let this sink in, to understand it. If we weren't trying, we'd have disowned you, right? But you have to understand that we cannot accept it overnight. It's going to take a long time, and quite frankly, sometimes it seems insurmountable."

And I said, "But, Mom, I need to be able to talk openly, to discuss my life, to talk about what's bothering me or talk about what I'm happy about, like a new girlfriend or whatever. I need to be able to discuss these things."

And she answered, "Well, no one is stopping you. Granted, the atmosphere is probably not so inviting, since we are uncomfortable with the entire topic. But no one is stopping you from saying anything. No one can shut you up if you have something to say. If you want to talk about those issues, it's up to you to bring them up. They are nothing that I know about and I'm not about to bring them up. And maybe if you did, even if we were resistant to talking about them, we might learn something."

When I hung up the phone, I cried even more, but they were happy tears because I realized things could change. My mother was right—a lot of this was still *my* job. I was expecting too much from them—they were already doing as much as they could. Now it was up to me, and quite honestly, I had to face the fact that maybe *I* was embarrassed about certain things about being a lesbian and maybe that was why I didn't bring them up. It was a real learning process.

Marilyn's mother was extraordinarily eloquent, and she helped Marilyn come to a realization that each of us comes to over and over again: Just when we think we've defeated our self-loathing it rears its ugly head. Self-loathing is so powerful that it can be responsible for darkening our lives even after we think we've seen dawn. Often we blame others for not "asking" when we haven't given them enough continuing information and encouragement. It is important for you to be vigilant about speaking about your life and the people in it. Each time you feel that your family is going back into the closet, think about what you may or may not have done or said to facilitate that. So go ahead and talk about your life.

"My sisters have never seemed eager to talk about my being a lesbian," says Anna, a twenty-one-year-old Boston college student.

> But I just keep plugging away, bringing it up as much as I can. My mother often tries to change the subject, but I bring it back. I think she used to get annoyed, in the beginning, and she kind of let me know that. Then she went through a change where she was trying to be more accepting and understand, and now, even though I know she probably doesn't want to talk about it, she'll have discussions with me just so she can be, you know, "a good mom of a lesbian."
>
> In time, I think she'll just be comfortable enough and interested enough that it won't be an act anymore. But we wouldn't have even come this far if I didn't keep talking about my life as a lesbian.
>
> My sisters now ask a lot more questions, even though one of them, the twenty-five-year-old, once said to me, "All you do is talk about being gay. Don't you think that maybe we don't want to hear it sometimes? Don't you have more to your life than that?"
>
> I told her that if she really thought about it, she would see that she was exaggerating. I don't *only* talk about being a lesbian, but it is a part of me and does come up, and I'm not going to hide it for her sake.
>
> But what really got her, I think, was when I explained to her how much she talks about being *straight* and how she probably didn't even realize it. How many times does she talk about some guy on a poster who's really hot? Or what about when she spoke about the guy she

went on a date with last week who dated her best friend? Or even when she and my other sisters are buying clothes and they say things like "That's a great outfit for dancing. Guys will go crazy over it."

After I told her that, my sister came to see that I really don't talk about being a lesbian any more than she refers to her heterosexuality. And she also came to see how important it is for me to talk about my being a lesbian whenever I can.

Step 9, Keeping the Discussion Going, is one step in the Outing Yourself process that you will continue indefinitely, for as long as you have a family.

YOUR WORST NIGHTMARE

It is impossible to know beforehand if the reality of your parents' and other family members' reactions will be your worst nightmare: complete and utter rejection and indefinite abandonment. In most cases, gay people who come out report that, over time, the results are far different from their initial imaginings. While the possibility exists that things will play out disastrously, it is our self-loathing that greatly exaggerates this possibility and makes us think it probable.

But all right, what *if* your parents—and/or others in the family—do *not* change after that first angry reaction? What if your worst nightmare comes true? What if your parents or other family members denounce you, reject you, disown you?

Whatever the chances of such an outcome, it is a possibility you should prepare for. Again, don't waste time envisioning this negative scenario, but be ready to handle it should it occur. Rejection by a family is a painful experience, and one that cannot be lightly dismissed.

"My father called me a lot of names, threw me out of his house, ordered my mother to pack up my things and not to ever contact me, and to this day my parents won't speak to me," says forty-year-old Garret, an Atlanta musician who came out to his parents fifteen years ago.

The pain and grief were terrible. I felt abandoned by the people I thought loved me. Luckily, I was prepared for it in terms of making sure it was physically safe for me and that I would have a roof over my head. I first thought about coming out to them when I was twenty-one, but I was still living in their house.

I don't know why I felt I had to do it, but I just needed to tell them. I couldn't lie anymore, even though back then being gay was much less accepted and they were not the most educated and understanding people by any stretch of the imagination. I knew they might react harshly, so I decided to wait for several years, until I was living on my own, so in that sense I prepared for it.

But preparing for it on a more emotional level, well, I don't know if you can ever be fully prepared for that. I had my friends, who really are like my family, and they really were behind me. I'm from a very large black family, and my grandparents and aunts and uncles were always important to me. That's why it was important to me to have older friends as well as younger—people with a lot of experience, who, for me, took the place of those older people in my family. They really comforted me.

My emotional state was crazy after my father threw me out. I had mood swings and changed my feelings a lot over time. I went from being angry to being sad and lonely to eventually not holding it against my parents. But no matter how I felt, or what stage I was in, I never once thought I'd done the wrong thing. I did what had to be done—I couldn't live in secrecy any longer.

I'd say it's like a grieving process. It's like when people say that no matter how much you prepare for the death of a sick person, you can never be fully prepared, and when the death occurs it's still a great loss and you have to grieve. Eventually, you get through it, but you need very much to mourn. It's the same with losing your parents in this way. You have to grieve and mourn, and let it pass after time. It's the only way to get through it.

In the end, I lost my parents as well as two of my brothers, but my sister and her husband are like my best friends. And my grandma and I still talk every week and she doesn't listen to a word my mother and father tell her. She loves me. And I have so many great friends of all ages who've stuck by me.

When people ask me about my family I say, "Yeah, I have a big, wonderful family." I'm not talking about my traditional "blood" family, but about the family I've made over the years that includes some of my relatives and lots of my gay friends and some straight. I wouldn't trade anything for them and I really don't believe anything is missing in my life.

I would say to people whose parents reject them that they have got to mourn and get it all out. Turn to your new family and be thankful that you have wonderful people in your life. This moment, no matter how difficult, will pass.

As Garret describes, preparing in a physical sense for rejection by your parents, brothers, sisters, or other relatives is easy compared to preparing emotionally. If your parents or other family members reject you outright and do not change over time, like Garret you will have to look to other relatives and to your gay and straight families of friends for support. You will have to mourn the loss. Facing reality is painful, but remember: Living in denial or bottling up the pain can be more detrimental to you in the long run.

If your parents have disowned you, you will have to assess your situation. With the help of your friends, who are more objective than you are, you must determine if your parents will evolve or are simply beyond reach of care and reason. If they are fiercely mired in their homophobia, then investing energy and time to make them change will only keep you filled with false hope and make the pain last longer.

Even after you have determined that your parents will not change, it is important that you not keep the pain inside or try to dismiss it too easily. Only after you have accepted that you did everything you could and that it is now out of your control—and only after you have felt the loss deeply and accepted it over time—will you be able to move forward.

TAKING NOTE OF THE CHANGES IN YOUR LIFE

Whether or not your parents and other family members have accepted your homosexuality over time, you have now altered your life profoundly. Not only have you told all of the closest, most important heterosexual people in your life that you are gay or lesbian, but you have kept the discussion going, continually challenging their attitudes about homosexuality and letting them see more and more of the hidden you. How wonderful that is after all those years of hiding! You undoubtedly feel a sense that there is no turning back, that being open about your

homosexuality is no longer an effort but rather second
nature.

At this point you will also begin to feel that you'd like
your family to meet some of the gay people in your life
who are closest to you. You'll feel that you are tired of living what have always seemed like two separate lives. And
now you know you are ready to move on to the next step
in the Outing Yourself process.

BRINGING HOME YOUR
GAY FRIENDS AND PARTNERS

After you have had that first talk with your parents and other family members, after you have kept the discussion going for some time, the most effective way to integrate your new openly gay self into your family and to integrate your family into your life is simply to live your life the way most heterosexuals do: Bring your friends and companions home to meet and get to know the family.

To further understand you and gay people in general, parents and family members need to see and meet your friends, companions, dates, and people with whom you might have longtime relationships. Often, they may be resistant to this, but after all you've been through, you must persist.

"I never thought my mother would accept *my* queerness, let alone anyone else's," recalls Stuart, a twenty-three-year-old retail clerk who lives in a small city in Maine, down the street from his mother.

But now she treats my lover as if he's part of the family. She has grown to love him. It took quite a while, and she didn't want to deal with it at first. For me to now bring new people home, people who were gay—well, I think in her mind I was fundamentally altering the family or something.

My father died several years ago and I'm an only child. My mother's brothers and sisters and their children, my cousins, are really the only family we have that gets together regularly.

When word spread to the rest of the family that I was queer, after I had told my mother and one cousin and an aunt, everyone pretty much accepted it fine. Several people in the family even came to me and offered support, as if they were acknowledging the pain that so many gay people go through because of prejudice. But they still all seemed to be operating by the "Don't Ask, Don't Tell" policy: They knew I was gay and accepted that, but it seemed they didn't want to see it "flaunted" in their faces, and that meant learning about my new queer life and meeting my friends.

I know it was that way for my mother. She tried being supportive of my being gay but when I decided I wanted to bring some friends home, she said she couldn't handle that. I just kept challenging her, asking her why, and letting her see that she was being irrational. One day I ran into her in a department store when I was with two friends, and that was perfect because she was able to see that they were nice people. Then I just brought them over to her house one night. She got to know them better, and now she's met many of my friends. When I started dating Rick, the man who is now my lover, I think it was easier for her to meet him because by then she'd met so many of my friends. There wasn't that wall set up and she took to him quickly.

There was a really marked difference in her acceptance of homosexuality in general after meeting my friends and my lover. She came to see that we weren't the evil and scary people that television and movies sometimes make gay men and lesbians look like. I think in the back of her mind maybe she unconsciously thought it was only a matter of time before I became a monster-child-molester-serial-killer-weirdo, or that maybe some of my friends were that. She would sometimes refer to those kinds of images in the media and it seemed to me they were something she was concerned about.

Whatever it was, now she's able to see *for herself* that so much of that stuff is so untrue and is ugly stereotyping.

Not only does meeting your friends and lovers break down stereotypes for your family and show them that gay people are normal, it also gives them a chance to be part of your life and to like and respect the people outside of your family who are closest to you. This in turn brings you closer to your family and helps them to better understand your homosexuality.

USE YOUR OWN JUDGMENT

This step will be different for everyone. In many cases it may not apply at all, or it may apply but at a later date. You may in fact move on to the next step, but come back to this step at some time in the future. If, for example, your parents live far away in a different town or city, it would not be convenient—and in some cases would seem strange—to go home suddenly and bring friends with you simply for the sake of introducing your parents to some other gay people. Depending on your family, even bringing straight friends home may seem odd. When your parents come to visit *you*, however, it is entirely appropriate to have them meet your friends. Behave exactly as any heterosexual in your family would behave. Don't force your homosexuality on the family in an awkward and uncomfortable way, but don't behave in a way that makes you less of a person than any other heterosexual member of the family. Be honest with yourself, however; don't let the vestiges of your inner self-loathing and your fear of confrontation cloud your judgment.

BRINGING FRIENDS HOME

Stuart lives in a small town, just down the street from his mother; it was natural for his family to meet his friends. You too may live near your family and be close with them—you may even live in the same house. Or perhaps you live farther away but have decided that you'd still like your family to meet some of your friends.

Which friend should they meet first?

"I decided to have my mother and father meet my friend Nora first," says Camille, a nineteen-year-old student from suburban northern New Jersey.

Nora is really smart and interesting, and above all, really understanding. She's been through this before with her own family and she knows how subtle you have to be, how the whole situation can blow up if you approach it the wrong way.

My friend Kathy is actually someone I'm a bit closer to, but she doesn't understand subtlety, to say the least. Actually, that's what I love about her. She's very political and very in-your-face, and nobody better even try to mess with her or they'll get an earful. But I thought she might not be best as the first of my friends to introduce to my family.

My mother and father took a while to come around. They're pretty conservative, and it took a lot of hard work on my part to get them from the point eight months ago where they just about threw me out of the house to the point where they really accepted me. I could have blown it all if the first person I brought home went off on some political diatribe.

Nora's just the opposite—polite and understanding and not very polemical. My parents needed to be disarmed in a way, and Nora's very good at that. Eventually, my parents did recently meet Kathy and some of my other friends, and actually, they get a kick out of Kathy and they now know she's closer to me than most of my friends. But I don't know if they'd have felt the same way about her—and about lesbians in general and about me—if I brought her home first, especially if she seemed threatening to them.

Like Stuart, you may find that you'd like to bring two friends home when you're finally ready to introduce friends to your family; or, like Camille, you may want to bring home one. Whatever the case, you'll have to use your own judgment in determining the person your parents meet first. It's important for parents to see the diversity of the gay community and to eventually meet all of your friends, but the *first* gay friends your parents meet should be those who will come across as comfortable and familiar. Remember, your parents are still coming to terms with your homosexuality, still prone to stereotyping and labeling. If you bring home someone who is confrontational, it will offer your parents an easy way out: They will be able to dismiss you, your homosexuality, and

your friends, and return to the comfort of their precon-
ceived notions. Your parents may also refuse to meet any
of your other friends if they do not like the first person
they meet.

When you get right down to it, the most provocative
person you can bring home is one who does *not* offer
them an easy way to dismiss your friends, but rather
someone who makes them so comfortable that they have
no choice but to accept your friendships. Later on, when
future introductions bring them to know a wide variety of
people, some of whom may be very different or confrontational, they will not be able to erase their first
impressions. Your parents will be gently pushed to view
the gay community just as they view the straight world:
filled with many different types, including some average,
polite, and quiet people.

EXERCISE 9: FIRST IMPRESSIONS

A simple exercise to help you choose who might be the
best person to bring home first requires you to once again
sit down in a quiet place with a pencil and a piece of paper.

Think about all of your best gay friends and write their
names down on the left-hand side of the paper. Look at the
first name you've written down and picture the person.
Think about his or her manner, appearance, tone of voice,
demeanor, and what kinds of things he or she talks about.

Imagine that you are your parents and other family members. First think of yourself as your mother, then your father,
then any others of your family who may be present. How
would you respond on first impression to this particular
friend (and remember, we are talking only of first impressions)?

Write down that impression, in one or two words, next to

the person's name. Go down the page and repeat this process with all of the names you have written down. Be honest with yourself: Just because you may love a particular friend doesn't mean that his or her first impression to parents will be a positive one.

When you have finished, look down the page at all of the words you have used to describe your friends from the point of view of your parents or other family members upon first meeting them.

Look for words that are neutral and not negative. Choose the friend or friends you feel have the best descriptions as those whom you will take home first.

WHEN, WHERE, HOW TO MAKE INTRODUCTIONS

Make the meeting between friends and family casual. Bring them home when other family members will be there with their own friends. Your birthday, in fact, is a perfect time to have family and friends meet, as it offers an opportunity that is not forced: The celebration of your day brings together naturally all the people in your life. The meeting can take place at your place, your parents' house, or at a restaurant or other public place.

Remember: The fact that you are choosing particular friends to bring home first does not mean that you should refrain from bringing others home, or that you hide certain of your friends from family view. Eventually, you will be able to bring home *all* of your friends, and your parents will see the spectrum of people who are now involved in your life.

WHEN YOUR FAMILY MEETS YOUR PARTNER

For many people, bringing home friends is not as important—especially when parents live in another city—as
having your family meet the person you settle down with
in a long-term relationship, whether you call that person
your lover, your partner, your boyfriend, your girlfriend,
or your longtime companion. It is only natural for you to
eventually have him or her meet your family, no matter
how far away they live, as this would *certainly* be true if
you were heterosexual. If you don't have a partner at this
time, you may want to move ahead in this book and come
back to this part of Step 10 after you're fortunate enough
to fall in love. Or you may want to keep reading and envision the day when you do bring someone special home to
Mom and Dad.

By the time your family meets your partner, they may
have already met some of your friends, and are thus
acquainted with some of the gay people in your life. This
will take some of the pressure off your partner. If, however, your partner is the first gay friend your parents are
meeting, he or she has the added burden of not only rep-
resenting the person you've chosen to bond with but also
standing in for all the gay people in your life. This could
be good or bad, of course, depending on the first impression your partner is able to make.

Unlike encounters between parents and friends, which
were more casual, the first time your family meets your
partner should be a little special. After all, if you were heterosexual and your family were meeting your significant
other it would undoubtedly be a special event. You'll
probably want to have your partner meet your parents
first, unless he or she has already met your siblings. The
meeting with Mom and Dad probably *should* take place at

a favorite restaurant over dinner. It might be a good idea
for your partner to buy a special little gift for your mother
and father. Good manners and the polite gesture—like
sending a thank-you note afterward if Mom and Dad
pay—will sweeten the event for everyone.

Decisions about how you time that first meeting will be
different for every gay person, depending on the customs
of his or her family—and for every gay or lesbian couple,
depending on the comfort level of both partners. If, for
example, yours is the kind of family in which heterosexual
members bring home a partner only when the relationship is very serious—or only when an engagement is
imminent—you might want to wait until both you and
your partner feel your relationship is equally serious. If,
on the other hand, heterosexuals in your family casually
introduce people they are dating to the family, you will
want to do the same—depending of course on the feelings of the person you are dating.

In these matters, do what you feel is appropriate to
both your family and your partner, and always in the way
you would operate if you were heterosexual. Again, always
make sure that your own fears of what could happen don't
cloud your decisions.

WHEN FAMILY MEMBERS DISAPPOINT YOU

You have been disappointed by your family before. You
may be disappointed in this as well, when you bring your
partner home.

"I was really living in a fantasy world," remembers
Donna, a thirty-six-year-old Milwaukee factory worker.

> I thought that once I brought my lover to meet my
> family four years ago, everything would be fine. They'd
> finally see that I *loved* just like they did. I thought it

would make them accept me more. Instead, they just treated me and my lover differently from the rest of the family. Until I raised a stink about it, my mother and father did not respect the relationship the way they respected my brothers' marriages—even though both ended in divorce all the while I've been with the same woman. That really got me mad.

My mother would not just automatically invite my lover to family gatherings she was having. And she would not set an example for what others should do either, so I would still sometimes get invitations to weddings to me alone, as a *single* person. And my brother once said to me, "We're having some people for dinner next Friday. Just family, so I don't mean to be rude." He meant that I shouldn't bring Pat. When I pointed out to him how insulting it would be if I had said that about his former wife, he got the message and was very embarrassed.

That's really what it's been about: I have to remain vigilant and constantly point it out to my family when they insult or offend me by not treating my lover like she's a part of this family. Usually, they get it when I tell them, but it seems I have to always be on guard.

Like Donna, you will have to be on guard too—not just about your family's sometimes offensive behavior but also about your anger. They are still overcoming homophobia and are bound to mess up. When this makes you angry, try to understand that most of the time they really don't mean to offend you—their behavior simply reflects what they have been taught all of their lives. Like Donna, however, don't allow your family to treat your relationship as less important than anyone else's. Speak up, as often as possible, not out of anger but out of concern. Your parents and other family members have, by now, come pretty far. They understand the pain you've gone through and are trying at this point to understand it further and even make up for it. More often than not, they will be conscious of your needs and try to right any wrongs, *but only if you approach them in a non-judgmental, non-accusatory manner.*

It's understandable that sometimes you will be so frustrated at what seems like such an obvious insult that you'll want to explode. But if you want positive and permanent change, however, not only should you try to be as non-confrontational as possible but you should also acknowledge to your parents or other family members that you are very happy about how far they've already come. Like you, they need constant reinforcement, and they don't have your family of gay friends—or this book—to encourage them.

"I was with my partner, Steve, at a Christmas dinner at my parents' house in Connecticut," recalls Karl, a thirty-one-year-old New York actor and writer.

I'd been out for three years and there had never been a problem. No one in my family is antigay and they all love me and respect me a great deal. But still, sometimes things happen.

At the table, in front of about fifteen people, my brother started talking about Christmases of the past, and about how he and my uncle and my other brother used to sing songs in which they'd change the words. They would videotape their performances in the basement, and come up and show the family later and everyone would get a kick out of it. My brother was referring to one song they'd sung about five years ago—the José Feliciano song "Feliz Navidad"—in which they changed one of the words in the refrain to *maricón,* which is Spanish for *faggot.* So the new refrain was "Feliz Maricón." I remember it well because it stung me so much.

And now he was reminiscing about it, and he was laughing and saying, "Oh, remember that song? Wasn't it great? That was one of our best."

Steve and I completely turned white. I was really offended. It was the first time I'd brought him— anyone—to meet my family. My uncle got it right away, and said something like "God, that was one of our low points. I was embarrassed about that one." But my brother didn't seem to get it at all. He just kept repeating himself and laughing. And no one else seemed to realize that two gay men were sitting there and he was saying an offensive word in another language.

I decided to try to change the subject. But later, when I was alone with my brother, I nicely but firmly told him how I felt, and I said, "You have been one of the most accepting and understanding people in this family and I really think you've come far in trying to deal with my being gay. I know it's not easy, and I really thank you for it. Look, this is not really a big deal—but it did bother me and it embarrassed me, and it made me feel not only like I was invisible but that my relationship is not respected either, since this person I love was also insulted. While I can accept it because you're my brother, I'm not sure he can."

My brother was beside himself—completely apologetic. He said that even though he knew what the word meant it just didn't register, and that this made him think about how often he uses words and doesn't think of their meaning and their power. He then went and apologized to Steve.

When you are upset about something that a family member has said or done, it's best to approach the person in a quiet place when the two of you are alone. If the family member has been understanding in the past of your homosexuality and has tried hard to be supportive, now is the time for that person to hear from you that you appreciate the support. By *prefacing* his complaint with a thank you, Karl was able to get through to his brother *without having his brother becoming defensive.* He also let his brother know that although he needed to still try harder, his efforts would not go unnoticed.

TAKING A BREATHER

After you have introduced your family to your friends and/or partner, and after you have learned to deal with their reactions and your disappointments, you should once again take a break, look back, and assess your situation. You have methodically and intelligently dealt with perhaps the most difficult tasks gay men and lesbians have to face. Your hard work will benefit you in all of your life, beyond only coming out of the closet. Not only have you learned how to talk honestly to people about intimate topics they would rather not discuss, but you've also learned how to check your anger and how to let people know—without alienating them—when they've disappointed you or offended you.

At this point, you probably should feel that you couldn't ever live in the closet again. You probably feel that you need to live this openly in every environment. When you realize that you'd rather not hide from anyone—even people at work, people who are not necessarily close to you but who nonetheless are constants in your life—you'll want to begin Part V of *Outing Yourself:* Outing Yourself to Your Coworkers.

PART V

OUTING YOURSELF TO YOUR COWORKERS

UNDERSTANDING AND ASSESSING THE SEXUAL NATURE OF THE WORKPLACE

For some of you, your heterosexual best friend may actually be a coworker; thus you may already have begun to out yourself at work. Even so, there are others at work who may be only acquaintances but who have established your company's overall environment regarding homosexuality. Everyone at work contributes to that environment. Unlike what some people might think, the average workplace is a sexual environment. Moreover, that sexual environment will almost certainly enforce heterosexuality.

"I was escorted around the agency [by my new boss] and introduced to some of the key people I needed to know," writes author James Woods in *The Corporate Closet* about his own first day at a new office, when he had been hired as a deeply closeted man.

First I met Sharon, who joined the company the week before. "I know what you're thinking," my boss chuckled to me, "but intrafucking is strictly against the rules." We moved on through the various offices and meeting

rooms, where I met many other employees. After each
ritual introduction, we exchanged vital statistics. They
wanted to know where I'd gone to college, where I
lived and if I was married. When I assured them I was
neither married nor "otherwise involved," one of the
men told me about the weekly singles night in the
cocktail lounge on the second floor. "I'll be there," I
said.

Woods, like many people, proceeded to cover up his
homosexuality for the purpose of fitting in and advancing
himself. In that way, heterosexuality is often institutional-
ized in the workplace, excluding and oppressing *homo*sex-
uals. It's a situation that causes much frustration, forcing
you to live a lie, which is why it is more beneficial for you
to be open at work. But first, you must make sure it is
safe, *that you in no way endanger your job.* If you truly feel
your job will be in jeopardy, you should not come out at
work. Depending on how overtly homophobic the work
environment is, you should perhaps start looking for
another job. Only *you* can accurately assess the situation
and decide what you should do. It may be unhealthy for
you to work in an environment that is openly hostile
toward you or forces you to disguise yourself as a heterosexual. If that is indeed the case, you are undoubtedly
under considerable stress and should perhaps seek outside
support and counseling.

We spend more time in our workplaces than just about
anywhere else. If you are ever to live a rewarding life, you
must work in a place where you feel comfortable. It's
understandable that you may not be able to leave your job
just yet, or perhaps you feel that although you may not be
secure in openly stating your sexuality, your work conditions are not *so* homophobic that you must make yourself
appear to be heterosexual. After reading through Step 11,

you will have to make up your own mind. For your own emotional well-being, it's healthiest for you to be out in every realm of your life. Unfortunately, no one lives in a perfect world and we all must exercise caution.

THE PERFECT COMPANY

The perfect company would be one where there is the following:

- a written policy against discrimination based on sexual orientation;
- a workplace diversity program that includes issues of concern to lesbians and gay men;
- a lesbian and gay employee group that is identified with the company's name and recognized and funded by the company;
- bereavement leave benefits in the event of a death of a gay or lesbian employee's domestic partner;
- health insurance that covers a domestic partner;
- a dental plan and a vision plan that extends to a domestic partner;
- pension/survivor benefits for a domestic partner;
- relocation assistance for a domestic partner;
- discounts on company products and/or services (or free use of company facilities) for a domestic partner.

According to studies performed by the Society for Human Resources Management and the Workplace Project of the National Gay and Lesbian Task Force, few companies offer all of these benefits to lesbians and gay employees. But more and more companies have one or more of these policies, and the list continues to grow.

Ed Mickens, editor and publisher of *Working It Out: The Newsletter for Gay and Lesbian Employment*, has published an indispensable book on the subject, *The 100 Best Companies for Gay Men and Lesbians*, which not only lists and rates the one hundred companies across the country that have the best policies for gay employees but also discusses strategies for coming out and creating change in the work environment. "Once you've started the coming out process, you're likely to find you're not alone," Mickens writes. "Reach out. Create a network; if possible, form a group. If it has a friendly social atmosphere, it's more likely to develop a healthy dynamic of its own."

In a company that is friendly toward gays, there is little reason for you to be closeted. Because of enlightened workplace policies in such companies, many people— both in management as well as among the employee staff—are often themselves gay and out of the closet, creating an atmosphere that makes it even more conducive to your coming out. In such companies homosexuality *is* included in the sexual nature of the workplace, and there is less enforced heterosexuality. The company itself often sends a message to straight management and to straight employees that homophobia will not be tolerated.

"I knew I'd been making excuses for years about not wanting to come out at work," says Kenneth, a thirty-four-year-old journalist who lives in California.

But the excuses were good ones. I could always tell myself that the company would not handle it well, that editors would discriminate against me, that I might lose my job. But soon after I moved to my current job, I knew I couldn't use those excuses because this company is very friendly toward gays, both in how it advocates to the outside as well as how it treats its gay employees. And there are openly gay people throughout the company.

But it was still not easy to do, to fight off everything inside of you that tells you to continue hiding. I had to make a commitment to myself not to hide and to stop pretending to be straight. Looking back, I see that I really could have come out at my other jobs. While they did not offer written protection, the companies were not antigay, and other people had come out and nothing happened to them. I used the lack of official protection as an excuse.

THE ANTIGAY COMPANY

On the opposite extreme from the perfect company is the antigay company, a company whose overt homophobia leaves you feeling targeted and fearful. At this kind of company, the owner, president, or members of the board of trustees or directors have made blatantly antigay remarks in public or supported antigay leaders, politicians, or political initiatives with money or endorsements. The company may have fired people because they are gay—which is still legal in all but eight states and in most municipalities—or it may even have a verbal or written policy against hiring gays. This kind of atmosphere empowers straight management as well as straight employees to voice their own homophobia, creating an overall work environment hostile toward gays. You might hear antigay remarks made at meetings or over lunch in the cafeteria, and people who are thought to be lesbian or gay may even be harassed—verbally or physically—and feel they have little or no recourse.

"My life was made miserable," says thirty-year-old Debbie, who until recently worked as a receptionist in an insurance firm in a small town in Kentucky.

I was subjected to so much hatred and harassment. Before that job, I worked in a factory, and the homophobia there was unbelievable. The foreman had put

up signs once on a bulletin board saying that he suspected there was some "homo goings-on" happening in
the men's room and that the company "would not tol-
erate such perverted activities" and would fire any
homosexuals it knew of. When the local paper investi-
gated, he told them that homosexuality was a sickness
and that he could not have mentally disturbed people
working for him. The whole time I worked there, people were calling me a "dyke" and "lezzie" right on the
packing floor. I didn't tell any of them I was a lesbian,
but they figured it out.

I thought that if I got out of that kind of job, with
guys like that who are rude and obnoxious, maybe I
wouldn't get harassed. So I took some courses at night
and brushed up on my office skills. Then I got the job
at the insurance firm and I was real happy at first.
Everyone was nice, smiled a lot.

But soon the harassment began in a different way.
They didn't have the guts to say hateful words to my
face. No, they'd write notes and leave them on my desk
when I went to lunch, mocking me, writing me love letters from imaginary women and using stereotypical
butch-dyke names for the women. I found all of this
even more degrading than what happened at the factory. At least those people were honest.

At the insurance company these guys in their suits
would smile and say good morning and then turn
around and do this nasty stuff anonymously and probably all laugh about it somewhere. I felt really demeaned.
I had to quit.

I got my current job—within a week of quitting the
insurance company, because I worked so hard looking—in a doctor's office, working for three women
doctors. They treat me with the respect and dignity
that any human being deserves.

THE BIG IN-BETWEEN

Most lesbians and gay men in fact work in an environment that falls somewhere in between Kenneth's and Debbie's. At the in-between company, while there might not be any written protection of gay people or any domestic partnership benefits to gay employees, there is no overtly hostile climate in the workplace toward gays. While in Kenneth's case there is no reason to stay closeted, in Debbie's case she had no choice but to leave the companies that were homophobic. She could not work in such environments and still have respect for herself. But at the in-between company, it's more difficult to figure out how or how much to come out. Assessing the sexual nature of the workplace in such companies requires more judgment.

"When I got my job, my mother was advising me that I shouldn't come out at work," says Jason, a thirty-two-year-old medical technician who lives in a suburb of Tampa, Florida.

> That was in total contrast to what my friend Billy said after I presented the facts to him soon after I started working at this hospital. I realized I just had to make up my mind for myself. There was never anything anti-gay said to me *per se*, but there have been homophobic jokes I've heard in my presence, and I sensed the usual kind of homophobia that is everywhere else.
>
> And yet, even though there's no written sexual-orientation non-discrimination policy, the hospital has responded swiftly a couple of times when employees have said that they were fired because they were gay. One guy got his job back. Still, my immediate supervisor is very conservative and I was afraid of what he might do if he knew. Some of the older women I work with are also religious, and I was just afraid. But I guess I couldn't hold it in too long.

That's how it is with me. It's hard for me to hide anything, and ever since I started coming out to people, my being gay has been the hardest thing for me to stay silent about. I don't go around shooting off my mouth about it, but I don't censor myself.

After a while everyone at work figured it out, and my boss even once brought it up during a discussion of gays in the military. He said, "This debate over gays in the military really raises a lot issues. It's the topic of discussion everywhere I go. Some of my friends have come down hard on the idea, you know, going to all the stereotypes about gays. But I told them they shouldn't jump on it so fast. I said that one of the guys who worked for me was gay. You *are* gay, aren't you?" I said yes, and he said, "Someone told me that, I forgot who. Anyway, I was wondering what you thought of this whole thing."

We had a good talk about it. I realized that he wouldn't have had his positive opinion on this issue— and told it to his friends—if he did not know someone gay. I also noticed that since my being gay had become known, the homophobic jokes among the guys at work stopped in my presence.

That really got me thinking: If you're waiting for the perfect environment to happen before coming out, if you're waiting for an environment where there are no homophobic jokes and everyone respects gay people— forget it. It doesn't actually happen *until* you come out, because people suddenly realize they know and like some gay people and can't talk that way in front of them.

As Jason describes, sometimes you can't be sure how people at work will react. While some people close to you might think it's a bad idea to come out at work, others will see no major problem. Only you can judge when and how you should come out. Be on guard: Self-loathing and fear will always try to suffocate your courage.

Because of everyone's wariness about coming out, assessing the workplace isn't easy. The following exercise might help you out.

EXERCISE 10: SCOPING OUT BOSSES AND COWORKERS

Think about all of the people in your work environment who matter to you, not only the people you like and respect or consider your friends, but *everyone* who has an effect on your work life and your paycheck. Include everyone from your boss to the person who works nearest you or sits next to you.

Write down all of the names of these people on a piece of paper, leaving a lengthy space under each one.

After you have written down all of the names, go back to the top and think about that person's interactions with you and how you are treated by that person. Now think about how that person would react if he or she learned that you were gay or lesbian—not how he or she would respond if you told him or her but how he or she would react if he or she learned, from someone else, of your sexuality.

Write down in detail the person's reaction and then describe how you think that person would treat you after hearing the news. Would the person stop talking to you? Confront you? Congratulate you? Or simply not treat you any differently?

If that person would react negatively and treat you in a negative manner, think about how that person might make your life difficult. What could he or she actually do? Write down the answers.

Go down the entire length of the page, doing the same under each name. When you have finished, take a good look at the page. While you may not find anyone who is over-whelmingly supportive, you will perhaps find a fair number for whom the disclosure simply doesn't matter.

If there are any people who would react harshly and treat you badly, think hard about how much of an effect they really can have on your life at work. How important is this person? If the person is your boss, for example, it is important, but if it is someone who is peripheral to your advancement, and to your immediate work environment, it may be less vital.

COMING TO CONCLUSIONS

From your list you will be able to evaluate the precise sexual environment of your workplace and how much of a risk you take by coming out. Also consider how your bosses or the company in general might handle any anti-gay harassment you might experience. Don't immediately write them off; employers generally don't want a contentious or hostile work environment and may be more sympathetic to your needs than you suspect, if only to keep the work environment free of conflict. Think about the people in Personnel or Human Resources, if there is such a department, and how they dealt in the past with conflict. Think about where support might possibly come from.

Once you have assessed the sexual nature of the workplace and thought a lot about how homosexuality would be viewed, you will know if it is time for you to wait things out, start looking for another job, or move on to Step 12 in the Outing Yourself process: Letting Coworkers Find Out.

LETTING COWORKERS FIND OUT

"Everyone at work knows and yet I don't really remember ever telling anyone at the office—you know, specifically coming out just for the sake of coming out," notes Stephanie, a thirty-seven-year-old Denver management consultant.

> I have always had my lover's and my daughter's pictures on my desk, and I have spoken about my home life often, and sometimes I have revealed my sexual orientation in passing, maybe when I'm having a conversation about vacations and I'm saying something like, "Well, my lover, Mary—I—you knew I was gay, right?—well, anyway, she and I went to Switzerland last year, and we thought it was a lovely place in the summer." Sometimes I don't even throw in the "you knew I was gay" phrase. Just mentioning my "lover" or "partner" by the first name of Mary usually does the trick.

Coming out doesn't always have to be a serious sit-down chat. The people at work are not so close to you or so important in your life that your disclosure is going to dramatically affect them. Thus, letting them find out in the same way you find out about their heterosexuality—through casual conversations, pictures on the desk, messages left, etc.—is often the best way to deal with it. There are actually many creative ways you can let them know.

"I remember that all the guys in the department store I work in thought I was straight," remembers Bettina, a twenty-three-year-old southern New Jersey retail clerk.

> They always tried to pick me up, using the cheesiest lines you can imagine. And it was really getting annoying. They were always trying to get me to go on dates with them, even after I said no a thousand times. I wanted to find a way to shut them up, but I knew if I said, "Look, I'm a lesbian," it would be like using it to make them stop, like it was a weapon or something, and that would just send the wrong message to them and make them believe all the stereotypes—you know, that all women who get angry about male advances must be lesbians.
>
> The plain truth is that they should not be treating *any* women, lesbian or straight, in the bothersome way they were treating me. A "no" is a "no." I decided they had to find out in a more natural way. When the company had a summer picnic, I thought it was the perfect time to bring my girlfriend. Those guys thought she was hot, I could tell. They were trying to pick *her* up. But after they saw her lying in my lap on the grass and saw me playing with her hair, they started thinking twice about things. It completely disarmed them because we were

not *saying* we were lesbians, we were just *being* lesbians.

And from then on I was not only left alone by them at work, but I swear I was completely respected. I was an out lesbian who didn't threaten them and scream at them but just lived her life, and I think it got through.

COMING OUT AGAINST HOMOPHOBIA

Of course, there are times—such as when a coworker who doesn't know about you is making antigay remarks—that you should consider making a point of coming out and politely but firmly explain why such comments are offensive to you. You may even need to go to your boss and report antigay harassment that you have been subjected to.

"I was always closeted in my office—never would let anyone know anything about me," says twenty-eight-year-old Howard, who is a bookkeeper at a North Carolina university.

> I was doing that whole self-loathing trip, thinking that being gay was no one's business but my own. In reality, I know I wasn't accepting being gay and so I couldn't understand anyone else accepting it. But I kind of changed when I began to receive threats from a coworker who was angry with me. First they were veiled, like, "I've got a secret on you and you'd better watch out." Then it was like, "I know you're a homo." I was so petrified. I thought it was the end of the world. In reality, it was the beginning. It was forcing me to deal with my closet.
>
> A friend of mine said, "You can't take that," and convinced me to go to my boss. The university is not con-

sistent on gay rights, and there's a lot of homophobia on campus. But I felt like I had no choice.

To my surprise, my boss was totally supportive and completely appalled at this coworker's behavior. He said he respected me immensely for confiding in him and realized that it was a lot for me to do because he knew I was such a private person. He reprimanded my coworker, who was so embarrassed he quit. My boss said he was thinking about firing him because of this incident anyway.

From then on, I was completely out in the office. Only that kind of incident would have gotten me out, but I'm glad it happened. I can't tell you how free and open I feel at work now.

MAKING IT FUN

You may find, like Howard, that you are forced to come out at work because of some pressing concern. But in a work environment where you feel secure, coming out can be leisurely and even sometimes fun.

"The women at work were always trying to match me up," says Wayne, a twenty-five-year-old mailroom clerk who lives in a Baltimore suburb.

They would show me pictures of their daughters, and their nieces and other people. And I was polite, and said, "No, I'm sorry, I'm just not interested, thanks." They even tried to get me interested in some of the girls at work.

Then one day this guy I was dating came to meet me at work, and he was really good-looking. They all started gossiping, saying, "Who's your friend? He's cute." I said, "He's my date," and they laughed, getting a kick out of it, thinking I was kidding.

For the next week, they kept kidding me about it, and I was thinking to myself, "Man, this is hilarious! I finally come out and they think I'm kidding!" When I left a stack of pictures on the table a week later, though—pictures that showed me and this same guy snuggling and kissing—they finally got the message. And it was pretty cool. I mean, they spent the next three weeks laughing at *themselves* for being so stupid.

You know, I thought that by letting them know I was gay they'd finally stop trying to match me up. But then, within three weeks, they started trying to match me up with *other gay guys* in the building, and with gay guys they knew. It was hilarious. They didn't change one bit. And, in a way, I like that.

ANOTHER ANGER-CHECK

As with every stage of the coming-out process, you must remember to check your anger, especially at work, where flare-ups and heated arguments could cost you your job. Not everyone is going to accept your homosexuality. Some people will react in a way that disappoints you. This is to be expected.

"I was angry because some of the guys who I considered close friends turned their backs on me," says Ike, a twenty-four-year-old Montgomery, Alabama, student who works summers as a camp counselor.

It really had me upset. Some people took it well but others just rejected me. I blew up on a couple of them, and they then reported me for insubordination. I had to just let it go—and I did. I soon came to the realization that if they couldn't accept it, they weren't good friends to begin with.

Checking anger is especially important if you are subjected to workplace homophobia. Some people may make
remarks and harass you. In the event that this happens,
it's important that you not respond in an equally angry or
immature way. The parties involved may just be threatened by your fierce response. If the harassment does not
stop, go to your supervisor and lodge a complaint. As Ed
Mickens suggests in *The 100 Best Companies for Gay Men
and Lesbians,* you should work to band together with other
gay people in the company if possible. Start your own
employee group if there isn't one. You can also turn to
others in the company who aren't gay but are supportive.
"Get out and around the company and start making
allies," Mickens writes, speaking not simply about
responses to homophobia but about organizing in your
company around gay issues in general. "They don't have
to be gay, just supportive or at least helpful. This isn't so
much about numbers as about cultivating assistance in
valuable places. You can keep it informal at this point
since you're still learning. Make the group's [or your] case
to the diversity manager, if there is one—that person
should be familiar with some concepts from literature in
the field. Ditto human resources and benefits, if they are
separate functions. Definitely talk to union representa-
tives, if any unions are involved (and if this won't completely freak out management)."

If you feel that none of these options are open to you,
and the harassment continues, you might have to face the
reality that it is time for you to start looking for another
job. It's important during coming out at work to keep
your options open always, in the event that something
goes wrong.

PREPARING FOR THE WORST

As when you've come out in previous steps, you should always be ready to manage the worst, even when you are envisioning the best.

"I really thought it wouldn't matter a bit," recalls forty-year-old Sheldon, an accountant who lives in a suburb of Washington, D.C.

> But the people in my previous firm were rabid homophobes—or rather the higher-ups at the firm were. Working there as an out gay person was made intolerable by these people. I had prepared for it, though. I had gone to a head hunter and let her know that I was in the market for a new job. That was just a precaution, but a smart one, since soon after I came out at work the remarks started and I was getting cut out of the loop.
>
> The head hunter eventually got me a job at a place where I was out of the closet in the job interview and they still hired me—the true test of tolerance! But even if things hadn't worked out so well, I wouldn't have been sorry about coming out at my previous firm. Living and working in the closet is not worth all the money and security in the world. I'd rather have been unemployed and starving for several months than have to endure that.

NO MORE HIDING

After you have come out at work, whether it is a positive experience or a negative experience that requires you to find another job, you'll feel that living honestly and decently is important to you and helps build your self-esteem. You'll realize that you exist, for the first time, entirely out of the closet, hiding yourself from no one.

It is at this point that you'll feel the need to go back and tie up any loose ends you might have left, fully completing the process of coming out—and moving on to Coming Out Every Day.

PART VI

COMING OUT
EVERY DAY

STEP 13

HELPING OTHERS
TO COME OUT

An important part of everyone's coming-out process involves helping and sponsoring other people on their journeys to outness and honesty. It offers each of us an objective look back and allows us to reevaluate our own process of coming out. It makes us see how we can affect others and enables us to see areas in which we might be able to come further.

"It wasn't until I helped a friend come out that I realized that I wasn't really being honest with myself," says John, a twenty-three-year-old aspiring film director who lives in Los Angeles.

> I wasn't fully out to many of the people in my own life. It's not until you look at other people closely that you see some of your own shortcomings in this area.
>
> I hadn't really spoken to my mother about my being gay since I told her about it. I had myself believing that she's accepted it fine, but really if she did I'd be more comfortable talking about my lover.

When I was helping my friend Michael go through his own coming-out process, and he was struggling with really integrating his gay identity into his family, I realized I hadn't integrated mine either. Here I was thinking I'd gone further than he had and helping him and stuff, and then it turns out that he was now going further than I did. I needed to do more work.

WAYS TO HELP OTHERS

There are many ways to get in touch with the coming-out processes of others, from helping closeted friends and acquaintances to joining a coming-out support group at a local gay community center or the similar organizations that exist at most colleges and universities. When you are finished with this book, one powerful way to help someone else would be to pass it on—as well as any other books on lesbian and gay heritage you may have purchased—to a closeted person.

You might want to write down the various ways available to you to help others to come out. You might also want to write down the names of some people who you know who are gay and closeted and might need help in coming out. Approaching these people and offering your help—without being pushy or condescending—will help you see how far you've come. You're now an expert—someone who can teach and counsel others. When the time is right, you might want to approach these people and say something like, "You know that I'm a lesbian [a gay man] and that I've gone through a lot in coming out. It was a difficult thing to deal with, but I got through it with the help of others and from drawing upon my own inner resources. I think I'm able to help other people with similar problems, and I feel a need and desire to help. If you ever need to talk, I'm here."

This approach is best, especially if the person is still deep in hiding, because you are making it clear that you know the person is closeted—which will probably only make such a person defensive—but you are still allowing him or her not to talk about anything upsetting. If a person is less closeted and has acknowledged to you that he or she might be gay, you can be more open about wanting to help him or her explore and deal with his or her closet. You'll have to use your own judgment, which by now should be less clouded with fear and internalized homophobia.

Whatever you do, be patient. Remember how hard it was for you to open that door to a freer and truer self. I'll be frank, however, and if you know my early writing for *OutWeek* magazine, you'll understand where I'm coming from: Once you're out, it's very hard to have sympathy for those who are still in.

BUILDING SELF-ESTEEM

For the rest of your life you will be part of a family of friends that includes someone who will be dealing with coming out. Helping others will continue to give you a sense of how far you've come and continue to build your self-esteem.

Maria, a thirty-five-year-old nurse who lives just outside San Antonio, Texas, says that helping her cousin come out made her realize how much of a pioneer she had been in her own family.

I'm the oldest daughter in a very religious Mexican-American family, and needless to say my family had a lot of problems with my being gay. My extended family wasn't so bad, actually. It's not like homosexuality is unheard of, and they knew of people who were gay. But

for my immediate family it was like, well, *forget about it!*
My father cried, and my mother prayed and prayed and
prayed. I thought they were going to throw me out.
One of my brothers almost hit me, he was so angry.

For the rest of the family, like I said, while it probably wasn't a big deal, because my parents were so upset,
they just stayed silent about it and only gossiped among
themselves and felt so bad for my family.

That was seven years ago. Now I bring my partner
home and they all love her. It's like she's a part of the
family. Yes, they adapted over time. Now my cousin,
who is twenty-one, has told her parents—my mother's
sister and her husband—that she is gay. And who do
you think is the first one to tell them it's all going to be
okay and to love and accept and understand her? My
parents!

The way the whole family is dealing with it is really
much different: Everyone talks about it out in the open,
with no gossiping and no feeling bad. It's part of the
modern world—that's their attitude. And they know
that it's no use trying to change my cousin, and that
you'll just waste a lot of time yelling at each other that
could have been spent loving each other.

I was the first person my cousin spoke to in the family, and I helped her go through the whole thing. I can't
tell you how good it made me feel, how much it kind
of validated all of these years of struggling to come to
terms with being gay. It made me see that I really broke
the ice in the family and that I had come so far and
really moved these people and pushed myself to be
open and proud of myself. That was a great thing for
me to learn, and I thanked my cousin for giving me the
opportunity to help her and learn more about myself.

REASSESSING YOUR OWN COMING OUT

Whether you help a member of your family, a friend, or someone you meet at a community-center support group or gay youth center, it's important for you to learn more about yourself by helping others. You are one of the best people to help others too, because you've gone through the process and probably now have many pointers of your own. Remember, you don't want to be preachy or pushy—you just want to be there for someone, to give him or her support and answer pertinent questions, just like the people in your own family of friends who helped you through coming out.

After you have helped one or more people come out, sit down and reassess your own coming-out process and the steps you took in this book. Look at how far you've come and what you've accomplished. Think about how you've been a pioneer for others, and think about your personal achievements. Visualize the ways in which you are different and a better human being. Think about the people you've helped and how afraid they were. Think about how long it's been since you were in that place. Pat yourself on the back. Reward yourself. Rejoice.

Then, after some time soaking in the good feelings, sit down again and, like John, critically assess where you still need to out yourself. There will always be some loose ends—because we're all human and because self-loathing never really goes away. Go back to the steps in this book. Which steps did you rush through and not fully complete? Which steps did you ignore? Which aspects of the steps are you in denial about, telling yourself you did them well and right, but knowing deep down that you could have done them more fully? How much did your own self-loathing keep you from not fully completing certain tasks?

When you have figured out where your deficiencies lie, go back and work on those steps. Push yourself to fully complete them in a way that makes you proud of yourself, no matter how difficult the task may be. When you feel that you have satisfactorily completed all the previous steps, you will be reaching the point when being out and coming out is a reflex as natural as breathing—not even something you have to think about. And you'll know it's time to go on to the last step in Outing Yourself.

NOT THINKING
ABOUT IT AT ALL

We never fully complete this last and final step—because
we will continue to come out every day for the rest of our
lives.

All right: You've told everyone who is close to you, and
all the serious sit-down chats are now behind you. So now
you'll simply lead your life, out of the closet, unconcerned
about what anyone—at home or at work—thinks. Right?
You'll run your life the way most heterosexuals do—not
thinking all that much about your sexuality and certainly
not thinking about how to hide it. Isn't that what you
always wanted?

"My life is so different from four years ago," says Elliot,
a forty-three-year-old man who owns his own restaurant
in Tacoma, Washington.

I feel so free. I remember that I would constantly think
about being a queer, of being different and being a
freak, because I was always trying to hide it. Now, it's
so out there, so much a part of the visible me, and yet I

rarely think about it. Everyone knows, and in any crowd of either old friends or new people—even in business—I never alter my conversations.

I remember people saying that those who were "out" were obsessed with their homosexuality. I now realize that all of that was just internalized homophobia. It's those who are "in" who are obsessed with their homosexuality—they're constantly thinking about it. The rest us have much more to do and think about. We're not obsessed. We're leading our lives, not thinking about it at all.

NOT THINKING ABOUT HIDING

Elliot's analysis about "not thinking about it at all" is razor-sharp. Of course he doesn't really mean that he *never* thinks about being gay; certainly we all think about being gay in a culture where there are so many messages telling us it is wrong. What he means is that most people who have come this far don't think all that much about *hiding* their homosexuality.

"I remember always watching what I was saying when I was with a group of gay friends and we were out in public, say, in a restaurant or at a movie," recalls Richard, a twenty-six-year-old New Orleans student.

Now, I don't care who hears anything I have to say, or what any of my friends say in public. In fact, now I love watching people's reactions when they're listening to us—they need to hear us talking about our lives, especially since we're always forced to hear them talking about theirs. And I realize that means I've come really far. I kind of laugh now when I meet new friends, people who are much more closeted, who spend a lot of time worrying about such things. I say to them, "Who

cares? You can't spend all your time in the closet, especially when you're out in public with your friends, worrying about who knows something about you."

Again, as both Elliot and Richard illustrate, it is only
those who are in the closet who are overly concerned with
homosexuality, not those who are out.

"I definitely used to buy into all of that way of thinking about gays who were out of the closet," recalls Sheryl,
a twenty-seven-year-old administrative assistant in Houston.

> I thought that the people who were out had this mad
> obsession with being gay and I would ask why they
> didn't cool it and live their lives and stop making such a
> ruckus.
>
> It's interesting because I'm a black woman whose
> parents brought her up teaching her about the civil-
> rights movement and Martin Luther King. They were
> always making sure I was on guard against prejudice.
> And yet I still didn't see how my logic about homosex-
> uals was so screwed up. Now I see that my being a les-
> bian and out about it and not caring about who finds
> out is *not* an obsession—it's just my way of life. And it's
> true, it's the ones who are hiding who have the obses-
> sion. They're so worried about their closet that I don't
> know how they could enjoy life. I said good-bye to the
> closet a long time ago, and I haven't thought about that
> nasty place at all.

COMING OUT EVERY DAY

By now you have probably come to the same conclusions
as Elliot, Richard, and Sheryl. You are probably very
proud and excited about how far you've come—and you

should be. You've done more work in outing yourself
than most gay people do in a lifetime—more, sadly, than
many ever will. You can now experience life's riches and
strive to reach your potential without the closet suffocat-
ing you. So it's important for you to remember again that
self-loathing will constantly work to undermine you. Try
to be on guard against it, even though it's something
you'll never rid yourself of. In this way, we are always
coming out, every day, always forced to beat down the
demon of self-loathing, and always required to stand up
for ourselves.

"I remember I once went to Miami, to South Beach,
which has become quite a gay-resort Mecca these days,"
recalls Bart, a thirty-six-year-old New York writer.

> I am way out at work, and have been out to my family
> for years. I don't ever hide my homosexuality. I was rid-
> ing in the taxi in Miami from the airport, having a con-
> versation with the driver, and we were really getting on
> well, talking about the beach and the weather and
> Miami in the old days.
>
> Then, when we pulled onto the street where my
> hotel was, there was a lot of traffic and he was getting
> frustrated. Two guys were running across the street in
> their Speedos, darting in front of the car, and they
> looked gay—at least to me—and obviously to the driver
> too.
>
> When they got in his way, he muttered, "Fucking
> faggots." I was floored, especially since I'd made friends
> with the guy. And I hated that I had to say something
> to him, but I felt I had to, or else I'd be behaving in a
> closeted manner—even though I was so out—and
> would have really felt like I'd felt in those days when I
> was hiding my sexuality.

I would have felt like a self-loather. It's like you can go back into the closet at any time, in any situation, and it seems you've always got to be busting out, every day, if you don't want people treating you like garbage. This was the classic example of that.

I gave the guy a good tip because he'd gotten me there quickly and was very friendly. And as I handed it to him I said, politely, but in a serious way, "I was very offended when you called those guys 'faggots.' I am a gay man. I don't know what you think about gay people, but you seemed to like me and enjoy talking to me and therefore it's not impossible for you to like and enjoy gay people. I'm sure you know and like many, even if you don't know they're gay. And really, you should be more careful about what you say because you never know when there is a gay person around. We could be anyone, anywhere."

He apologized profusely, saying he wasn't even aware of what he'd said and that he was real sorry. I said, "I understand, just don't let it happen again." And he was like, "You got it. You're right."

I felt good about myself that day, about doing that little thing, and I knew I had to do it because if I didn't I would have felt bad about myself, angry with myself for letting him get away with it.

HONORING YOUR DIGNITY

Bart's forthright action illustrates the idea of "coming out every day" and how, in order for you to live with dignity, you must be able to politely but forthrightly stand up to people whose homophobia adversely affects you. Of course, there are no hard-and-fast rules about this, and you will have to use a fair amount of case-by-case judgment. Your safety is first and foremost: If a gang of violent teenagers is making homophobic remarks in your presence and you are all alone, it is obviously unwise for you to confront them verbally. Homophobia is rampant, and it sometimes manifests itself violently. We must all sometimes hold our tongues, and such situations cause stress and make us feel cowardly. But if you do rise to the occasion and fight homophobia in those situations where it is safe for you to do so—such as when Bart gave a cab driver a gentle lecture—you will be able to tell yourself that, unlike many other people who cower in fear and never speak up, you are honoring your dignity in the best way you can.

Speaking up in those situations in which it is safe to do so will balance those situations in which you are not able to say anything or those situations in which you are simply not having a good day and/or don't have the energy to speak up. Do it when you can, and don't beat yourself up for failing to do it when you can't.

LIVING OUT OF THE CLOSET

When you are able to tell yourself honestly that you do the most you can to safely but effectively battle the forces "out there" that make you feel bad, as well as the forces inside that mire you in self-loathing, you'll know you have successfully completed the Outing Yourself process.

When you are able to help others deal with their own closets without fear and apprehension, and when you serve as a role model for other people who are struggling, you'll know that you have successfully completed the Outing Yourself process.

And when coming out is no longer a daunting, burdensome experience but something empowering and liberating that you do every day of your life simply by *living* out of the closet, you'll know you have successfully completed the Outing Yourself process. Congratulations, and remember to work every day to fight self-hatred, and to truly, profoundly love who you are.

ACKNOWLEDGMENTS

I cannot express enough thanks and appreciation to the scores of lesbian and gay men across America who filled out questionnaires about their coming-out experiences or gave me lengthy interviews, allowing me to delve into the most personal aspects of their lives. At different stages of outing themselves, they each spoke from the heart and offered their insights so that many others could learn from their triumphs as well as from their mistakes. Their stories were invaluable to the creation of this book.

I also owe a great debt of gratitude to the many lesbian and gay psychotherapists, psychologists, psychiatrists, and counselors whom I consulted personally on this project or whose bodies of published work guided me in creating this step-by-step program. Their pioneering work, often met in the past with great hostility by their heterosexual (and often homophobic) peers, has made it possible for books like this one to be published.

As usual, my talented editor and friend, Mitchell Ivers, worked his magic, shaping this book and helping me to

speak in a clear voice. I was privileged to have the guidance of the respected editor David Groff, whose input
also made a profound difference. I am also grateful to my
faithful agent, Jed Mattes, who never ceases to instill me
with confidence. Many thanks as well to Paul Hamann,
who assisted me in jump-starting this project.

Last, I'd like to thank my own family of friends (you all
know who you are), who have always been there when I
needed them, and whom I love dearly.

ABOUT THE AUTHOR

MICHELANGELO SIGNORILE is the author of *Queer in America* and a columnist for *Out* magazine. He has also written for *The New York Times*, *The Village Voice*, *USA Today*, *The Advocate*, the *New York Post*, the New York *Daily News*, *People*, and *The Face*. He is a graduate of the S. I. Newhouse School of Public Communications at Syracuse University, and he lives in New York City.

ABOUT THE TYPE

The text of this book was set in Janson, a misnamed typeface designed in about 1690 by Nicholas Kis, a Hungarian in Amsterdam. In 1919 the matrices became the property of the Stempel Foundry in Frankfurt. It is an old-style book face of excellent clarity and sharpness. Janson serifs are concave and splayed; the contrast between thick and thin strokes is marked.